ENGLISH SEVEN TO TWELVE

D. Hughes and A. Josephs

Illustrated by T. Wanless

COLLINS: GLASGOW & LONDON

© 1980 D. Hughes and A. Josephs
0 00 314320 1
First Impression 1980
Printed in Great Britain
by William Collins Sons & Co Ltd
Glasgow

Notes for teachers

This book is the fourth of a series of five, the aim of which is to provide teachers of the 7–12 age group with a structured scheme for the teaching of a wide range of basic English skills. One of the main features is the use, as stimulus material, of extracts from recent children's fiction of acknowledged high quality.

The book follows the same pattern as the first three books in the series. It has thirty Units, each of which fits into an overall pattern, whilst having a distinct unity of its own, based on six sections closely linked to the initial stimulus. Many of the sections offer two types of related tasks. The presentation is practical and each Unit is completely contained within a four-page spread. A feature of Book 4 is the inclusion of reference skill work linked to both the picture and the passage.

Unit pattern

1 The opening passage (mainly prose but sometimes verse) is the key to the whole Unit and each of the other sections is closely linked to it. A major aim is to excite interest in the books from which the passages are taken, and the book-list on page 126 will act as a valuable class library list.

2 The comprehension questions ('Understanding'), as well as testing thorough and accurate reading and summary skills, also present opportunities for individual thought and opinion. One particular intention has been to allow the less able child the chance to offer answers which are acceptable if not as elaborate as those provided by the more able.

3 'My own work' uses the opening passage as the stimulus for creative writing. Again the aim has been for every child to be motivated to find a successful response.

4 The picture is intended primarily to act as the stimulus for a creative response as well as for oral activities. The link between the picture and the passage is deliberately a loose one, to encourage a wide range of response from both teacher and child.

5 In each Unit work concerning reference skills is provided, linked to both the picture and the passage, but **not** intended to prevent the creative and discursive use of the picture. The work should prove interesting and valuable in promoting the development of such skills as listing, classifying, labelling, making headings and notes, thus providing practice in the organisational skills needed in topic and project work. Questions on the use of dictionaries, encyclopaedias and other works of reference are included, with the assumption that the children will have access to good examples of such books.

6 This section is a constant factor, in testing and revising the basic skills of handwriting, vocabulary, sentence structure, punctuation, spelling etc.

7 The last section ('Language') introduces new language skills or reinforces others already introduced, both in this book and in the previous books of the series. Technical terms are used in this book and a key to the skills being tested is included in the list of contents. In this section, as in sections 2, 5 and 6, a systematic approach is followed, based for the most part around patterns of five or ten questions. Such a pattern will aid both sentence and composition structure.

Contents

Reference skill	Principal language skill
Observing, classifying and listing	The alphabet
Encyclopaedia work and note-making	Nouns, verbs, adjectives
Relevance in making comparisons	Sentence structure
Listing and precise detail	Prefixes with common roots
Organising and planning	Letter writing and layout
Research for biographical information	Direct speech
Use of dictionary – specialist word list	Apostrophes
Using instructions to make information sheet	Paragraph structure
Advertisements – relevant detail	Nouns
Definitions and dictionary work	Emphasis
Research, plan-design and labelling	Verbs
Research into origins of names	Pronouns
Note-making	Adjectives
Accurate plan-design and labelling	Similes
Research into events and dates	Questions
Map and atlas work	Prepositions
Library research – information sheet compilation	Adverbs
Precise information and sketch-map work	Sentence structure
Accuracy in comparison of maps	Compound nouns and hyphens
Notice-making – relevant information	Conjunctions
Time-chart and historical research	Inverted commas
Close observation of pictorial detail	Prefixes and suffixes
Classifying in tabular form	Adverbs and adverbial phrases
Research and compilation of booklet	Sentence formation
Word derivations – use of dictionary	Sentence formation
Relevant information for reference book	Paragraphs
Research and compilation of booklet	Parts of speech
Accurate map-making and atlas work	Versification
Project work and book design	Revision
Diary information and construction	Revision

unit 1

At school in Victorian England

It was on a May morning when everything was bright and shining outside, and Ellen was aching all over with having to sit still at school. She was supposed to be writing her copies at the long desk under the window while other children were called up to Miss Higgs' table to read. The babies were gabbling their alphabet, first forwards, then backwards, over and over again, and everybody was busy except Ellen. She had written 'Procrastination is the thief of time' four times, each time worse than the one above, and had no wish to write it a fifth. So she poked Eliza Moon with her elbow.

"Why do you write with your tongue sticking out? Our old cat does that if you tickle behind his ears. Shall I tickle behind your ears?"

But Eliza wrote steadily on.

"Or I'll ink your tongue if you like, so's you can write with it." Ellen jabbed her pen into the ink pot, dragged it out full and pointed it at Eliza, who gave a bleat and jerked herself away.

"Who is that making a disturbance down there? Ellen Timms. I thought so. Come out to the front with your copybook." Miss Higgs took out her ruler meaningly, and laid it in front of her.

Everybody watched while Ellen went up. The babies, still gabbling ZYXWV, stared at her with huge round eyes; the writers held their pens poised over their copies; the group round Miss Higgs' table, clutching their books, fell back to let her pass.

"Disgusting, as I thought," said Miss Higgs, glancing at the copy, in which 'procrastination' had been spelt four different ways, and which was lavishly spattered with blots. Then Miss Higgs produced the label 'Empty vessels make the most sound' – it was worn by Ellen more than by anybody else in the school – and pinned it to her back.

But Ellen scarcely noticed this time, for she was staring out of the window behind Miss Higgs' back.

from 'Ellen and the Queen' by Gillian Avery

Understanding

1 What was Ellen supposed to be doing?
2 What was Ellen actually doing?
3 What were the infants doing?
4 What was Miss Higgs doing?
5 Why do you think Eliza had her tongue out when she was writing?
6 Why did Miss Higgs call Ellen out to the front?
7 Why do you think Miss Higgs took out her ruler?
8 How was Ellen punished?
9 How do you know Ellen was quite often in trouble at school?
10 Why did Ellen ignore the punishment this time?

My own work

A   The passage describes one of Ellen's bad days at school. Describe a day that you remember when everything seemed to go wrong. Describe what you felt, as well as what happened.

B   Now describe a day you remember with pleasure because everything went right.

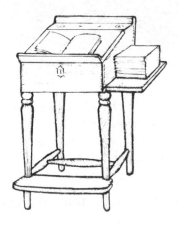

The modern classroom in the picture is probably very different from the Victorian school that Ellen and Eliza attended. Write the heading 'A Modern Classroom', look closely at the picture and make a list of all the things you notice that would fit the heading, for example the type of furniture, display, room arrangement, etc.

You may wish to include things that are in **your** classroom but not in the picture.

Handwriting

In Victorian schools children were often asked to write out sayings that were meant to improve their behaviour. Below is a list of ten old sayings. The first and last ones are from the passage.

Write out the sayings in your best handwriting, to make a notice for the wall in Miss Higgs' classroom. Find out what each of the sayings means.

1 Empty vessels make the most sound.
2 Practice makes perfect.
3 Where there's a will there's a way.
4 When in Rome do as the Romans do.
5 The pot shouldn't call the kettle black.
6 Two wrongs don't make a right.
7 Waste not, want not.
8 Do as you would be done by.
9 You can't eat your cake and have it.
10 Procrastination is the thief of time.

Language

The infants in the Victorian school were saying the alphabet over and over again, forwards and backwards. It is just as important today to know the alphabet well, especially when using a dictionary, an encyclopaedia or an index.

Answer these questions about the alphabet.

1 What does **alphabetical order** mean?
2 Write down the surnames of ten people in your class and put the names in alphabetical order.
3 If the letters of the alphabet were numbered 1–26, which numbers would the five vowels have?
4 Which letters would be numbered 4, 8, 12, 16, 20, 24?
5 The names Ellen and Higgs both include double consonants. Name five more consonants that are sometimes found as double letters.
6 Name five consonants that are sometimes followed by the letter h.
7 Which consonant is always followed by the letter u?
8 When the infants in the passage were saying the alphabet backwards, which five letters would they say after the letter v?
9 Which word in the last sentence of the passage would come first in a dictionary?
10 Which word in the last sentence would come last in a dictionary?

unit 2

Choosing a present

Each summer, when he went to stay with her, Aristide's grandmother would buy him *one present*. He was allowed to choose whatever he wanted. Because there were so many nice things in the shops it took Aristide a long time to make up his mind what to have. By the end of the first week, in which he looked in the shops at the boats to sail and giant rubber balls and fishing-rods, he had decided that what he wanted most of all was a shiny, plastic mattress which you could blow up and float on in the sea.

Together with his grandmother Aristide went to the shop which sold them. They were hanging up outside; blue-and-white, red-and-white, and green-and-white. Some of them had a piece of clear plastic, like glass, in the pillow part, so that when you lay face down in the water you could watch the fishes swimming in the sea.

The stout lady and the small boy stood for a long time on the pavement outside the shop looking at the lovely shiny mattresses. At last Aristide said: "Blue". It was a big decision.

As if by magic, as soon as Aristide had spoken, the man whose shop it was came out of it and with a long stick unhooked the blue mattress from where it was hanging.

Aristide's grandmother gave the man the money. Aristide gave his grandmother two kisses, one on each cheek, to thank her for buying him the present, and carrying it together they walked through the streets to the little villa with the frilly curtains where they were to have chicken in cream for supper.

All night the shiny blue mattress lay at the foot of Aristide's bed.

The very last thing he wished before he went to sleep was that the next day would be hot enough for his grandmother to let him use it.

from 'Aristide' by Robert Tibber

Understanding

Explain why each of the following is important to the story told in the passage.

1 Aristide's grandmother
2 the shops in the town
3 the shop that sold plastic mattresses
4 the piece of clear plastic
5 the blue mattress
6 the shop-keeper
7 the long stick
8 the little villa
9 Aristide's bed
10 the weather

My own work

A   Aristide and his grandmother were staying in a holiday resort at the sea-side. Describe a sea-side town **you** have visited, mentioning the beach, hotels, amusement places, shops and cafés etc. If you haven't visited such a place, imagine you are describing the place where Aristide was staying.

B   Many people keep a diary of what happens each day during their holiday. Write a diary of the week Aristide spent with his grandmother. It may help to think of some of the things **you** have done on holiday.

11

Aristide hoped to use his plastic mattress to watch fish swimming in the sea. Scientists sometimes descend far under the sea in an observation bell, like the one in the picture. Through the window they gain information about many types of sea creatures.

Below are the names of ten sea creatures. Find information about each one from an encyclopaedia or reference book. For each creature write down the information you think is important.

seahorse	dogfish	prawn	salmon	killer whale
angel fish	octopus	conger eel	dolphin	stingray

Words

Look at the word <u>present</u> in the second line of the passage. It means a gift but the same word can also mean <u>being here</u>. In a dictionary these two meanings would be shown like this:

present: 1   a gift
       2   being here

Here is a list of ten more words that have more than one meaning. For each one write out two meanings as they would be shown in a dictionary.

fair	spell	round	spring	bank
sink	right	scale	pupil	batter

Language

All these questions are about **nouns, verbs** and **adjectives** used in the passage.

A   1   Write down two **nouns** that name people.
      2   Write down two **nouns** that name things in the shops.
      3   Write down two **adjectives** that describe the plastic mattress.
      4   Write down two **verbs** that say what Aristide would do with the mattress.
      5   Write down two words ending in <u>ing</u>, formed from verbs.

B   Now find in the passage five more nouns, five more verbs and five more adjectives.

The hen that turned white

Meanwhile, out in the henrun, Pecker was getting very excited and curious. The other hens were quite content to scratch round and jump up at the cabbage stalk that was hanging from the wire roof – but not Pecker. She clucked and pecked and scratched at the trap door. When Ronnie heard her he said, "Let's let her in and show her round. She won't half be pleased at all this white!"

He lifted the trap door and Pecker came squawking in.

As soon as she was inside she made straight for the half-full bucket of whitewash and jumped on to the edge of it.

"Get off, Pecker! Get off!" said Ronnie excitedly. "Get off that bucket!"

But Pecker didn't get off – she got in! And head first, too! Oh, what a shock she had – instead of a nice breakfast of meal there was cold, clammy, nasty whitewash! She plunged about with her wings and her feet and shook her head and blinked her little black eyes, and squawked and squeaked like a peacock before a thunderstorm.

"Golly!" said Lecky. "Now we've done it! Let's tip her out." And he tilted the bucket and managed to tip all the remaining whitewash – it was the thick stodgy part from the bottom, too – on to poor Pecker's back.

As soon as she was out she ran wildly round and round the henhouse flapping her wings and tail feathers. Then she went through the trap door and back into the run.

The other hens thought some strange animal – or perhaps a chicken ghost – had got into their run. They couldn't recognize their old black friend under all that whitewash. Poor Pecker! She stood blinking in the sunlight and trying to find her bearings.

Elsie and Doris and the Old'un all went into a huddle at the end of the run. Then all at once they seemed to make up their minds – and they charged at the whitewashed Pecker!

They flapped their wings at her, climbed on to her back, and pecked her comb and her legs, and no amount of squawking from Pecker could convince them who she was. Every time she flapped, bits of whitewash came off her feathers and settled on to the other three; so that by the time Ronnie and Lecky got round to the run there were three speckled hens and one white one.

from 'Painter's Mate' by Susan Hale

Understanding

1 What do you think Ronnie and Lecky were doing?
2 Why do you think they let Pecker into the henhouse?
3 How did Pecker actually get into the henhouse?
4 Why do you think Pecker got into the bucket of whitewash?
5 What effect did the whitewash have on Pecker?
6 How did Lecky make things worse?
7 How did Pecker get out of the henhouse?
8 How did the other hens react when they first saw Pecker?
9 Why do you think they charged at her?
10 What was the effect on the other hens of their fight with Pecker?

My own work

A Ronnie and Lecky seem the sort of boys who mean well but still get into mischief. Write a story about another job they tried to do which went wrong.

B Now describe a job **you** have done at home or at school.

The hens in the picture are battery hens and they lead a very different life from free range hens like Pecker.

Use both the picture and the passage to list five ways the lives of these two types of hen are different. Give your list a suitable heading. At the end of the list write a few comments giving your own opinion about these two ways of keeping hens.

Words

A   All the following **verbs** in the **past tense** can be found in the passage. They all describe the action clearly. Write down each of the verbs and in each case say who was doing the action.

> clucked   pecked   scratched jumped plunged
>
> squawked squeaked tilted   charged flapped

B   Now here is another of Pecker's adventures. Write out the story, choosing a suitable word of your own for each of the ten gaps.

One day Pecker and the other hens escaped from the henrun. They _____ through a hole in the wire and _____ down the path towards the pond. Pecker saw her reflection in the pond and _____ very angry. She _____ straight into the pond, and had another terrible shock! She _____ wildly out of the water. She _____ and _____ like a dog that has been stung by a bee. Luckily Ronnie and Lecky soon _____ her, _____ her and _____ the hens back to the henrun.

Language

A   There are many different ways of building up good sentences. Make a list of the sentences in the first three paragraphs of the passage. Answer the following questions about **each** sentence.

1 How many actions are described? Which words are used?
2 Which words (if any) are used to show **when** and **where** the actions happened?
3 Which words are used to name the boys or hens?
4 Does the sentence make complete sense on its own?
5 Are there any words (like <u>Then</u> or <u>Next</u>) that could have been left out?

B   Now look at the ten sentences that make up the last four paragraphs of the passage. Number the sentences 1–10 and for each one write some comments about how long it is, the words that are used and the way it is linked to the sentences before and after it.

Mr. Nobody

I know a funny little man,
  As quiet as a mouse.
He does the mischief that is done
  In everybody's house.
Though no one ever sees his face,
  Yet one and all agree
That every plate we break was cracked
  By Mr. Nobody.

'Tis he who always tears our books,
  Who leaves the door ajar.
He picks the buttons from our shirts,
  And scatters pins afar.
That squeaking door will always squeak –
  For prithee, don't you see?
We leave the oiling to be done
  By Mr. Nobody.

He puts damp wood upon the fire,
  That kettles will not boil:
His are the feet that bring in mud
  And all the carpets soil.
The papers that so oft are lost –
  Who had them last but he?
There's no one tosses them about
  But Mr. Nobody.

The fingermarks upon the door
  By none of us were made.
We never leave the blinds unclosed
  To let the curtains fade.
The ink we never spill! The boots
  That lying round you see,
Are not our boots – they all belong
  To Mr. Nobody.

Anonymous

Understanding

A   Make a list of ten mischievous things Mr. Nobody does in people's houses.

B   1   Explain why the name <u>Mr. Nobody</u> is a very suitable one.
      2   What does the word <u>Anonymous</u> mean at the end of the poem?
      3   Why is <u>Anonymous</u> a suitable name for the author of this poem?

My own work

A   Mr. Nobody is obviously at work in everyone's house. Write down five things he does in **your** house. Remember that Mr. Nobody is blamed for things that go wrong.

B   Now write another verse for the poem, including some or all of the list of things you have written in Part A.

     Here are some ideas about the rhyme and rhythm to help you make your verse like the other four.

1   Each verse has eight lines.
2   Lines 1, 3, 5 and 7 are the same length, each having 8 syllables.
3   Lines 2, 4, 6 and 8 are slightly shorter, each having 6 syllables.
4   Lines 2 and 4 rhyme.
5   Lines 6 and 8 rhyme.
6   The last line of each verse ends with <u>Mr. Nobody</u>.

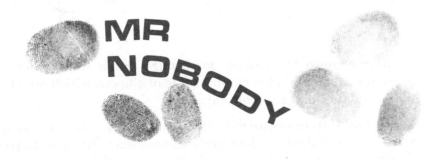

The poem blamed Mr. Nobody for leaving things lying around. The picture shows a man hidden behind a pile of objects, which are perhaps ready for an auction or jumble sale.

Before a sale, an **inventory** is often made, a list of the goods for sale with a few details about each of them. Choose ten of the objects you can see in the picture and make a suitable inventory of them. Put a heading 'Inventory of goods for sale'.

Spelling

A   To make the **plural** of most **nouns** we add <u>s</u> to the **singular**. For example, <u>books</u> in the second verse of the poem is the plural of <u>book</u>.

Write down ten plural nouns from the poem, all of which form the plural by adding <u>s</u> to the singular.

B   Not all plurals are formed just by adding <u>s</u>. For example look at the word <u>feet</u> in the third verse of the poem.

Here are ten groups of three nouns. Each group of nouns forms its plural in a different way. Write down the plural of each word and add another word to each group. Questions 8–10 need special thought!

1	table	chair	classroom
2	box	brush	mattress
3	baby	lorry	dictionary
4	donkey	journey	valley
5	leaf	shelf	wolf
6	gentleman	postman	policewoman
7	hero	potato	volcano
8	sheep	deer	aircraft
9	tooth	mouse	child
10	scissors	measles	athletics

Language

A   The word <u>nobody</u> is the main word in the poem. <u>No</u> is a **prefix** attached to <u>body</u> which is the **root** of the word. Other words with the same root but a different prefix are <u>anybody</u>, <u>somebody</u> and <u>everybody</u>. Each of the four words has a very different meaning.

In the following conversation put the correct word in each space.

"I heard _____ knocking at the door."
"Did _____ else hear the knock?"
"_____ else in the house was watching television."
"So _____ heard it except you?"

B   Now make up two more conversations, each containing four speeches. The first conversation should include the words <u>nowhere</u>, <u>anywhere</u>, <u>somewhere</u>, <u>everywhere</u>. The second conversation should include the words <u>nothing</u>, <u>anything</u>, <u>something</u>, <u>everything</u>.

21

A warm welcome

By the time Paul arrived the following day the house really was smothered in welcome notices. Etta had had plenty of time to make them. She had started off with very elaborate ones with pictures of Paul arriving with his suitcases and all the Milfords standing on the step to greet him. There was one on the wall over the table with a picture of all four sitting down to a huge meal big enough for at least a dozen people. There was a simply splendid arrangement in his bedroom with letters so big that the notice covered the whole of one wall. Then she ran out of ideas and made half a dozen with just the word WELCOME and put these in all sorts of unexpected places. And finally she had the idea of hanging a clothes line outside the house from one bedroom window to another and pegging sheets of paper on the line. Each piece of paper had one letter on it and the whole message read PAUL ARRIVES TODAY HURRAY HURRAY HURRAY.

Paul got out of Mr. Truman's car and saw this notice first. He stood and read it slowly. Mr. Truman got his bag out of the back and then looked up. "Red-carpet treatment," he said.

Paul looked puzzled but didn't say anything more just then. They went in. There was a feverish air about the house and Paul felt it straight away. Mrs. Milford didn't look any different but her voice had a strained sound and there were little lines round her eyes as if she was worried about something. After she had greeted them both she told Paul to go and find Etta.

"She's in such a state I sent her out to clean her rabbit hutch," Mrs. Milford said to Mr. Truman. "Go and find her, Paul; you know where to go, don't you?"

Paul looked at Mr. Truman.

"I'll give you a shout before I leave."

"All right," Paul said and went off.

Immediately Etta saw him she started talking and she went on getting quicker and quicker so that Paul coudn't get a word in. Even when she asked him questions she didn't wait for the answers. She told him about the letter that had come and what she had said to her father and what he had answered. She told him about the special lunch Mrs. Milford had prepared for him and about the flowers in his room and about how she had spent the whole morning making welcome notices.

from 'Paul and Etta' by Richard Parker

Understanding

A   For each of the following write a **short** answer and then explain **why** you chose that answer.

1 Were the Milfords expecting Paul?
2 Had Paul been to the house before?
3 Was Paul there just for the day or for a longer stay?
4 Was Mrs. Milford glad Paul had arrived?
5 Had Mrs. Milford made any special arrangements for Paul?
6 Had Mr. Milford been involved with Paul's visit?
7 Was Etta excited when Paul arrived?
8 Was Mr. Truman going to stay with Paul?
9 Was Paul excited about his visit to the Milfords?
10 Who do you think Paul was?

B   Etta had prepared several types of welcome notices for Paul. Make a list of them and say what is the main information the passage gives you about each one.

My own work

A   Look back at the answer you wrote to question 10 in Part A of **Understanding**. Write a story, involving Paul, Etta, Mr. and Mrs. Milford and Mr. Truman, that describes what led to Paul's visit to the house.

B   Now follow up your story and the passage with another story that describes what happened during the rest of the day.

Both the passage and the picture are concerned with the excitement of a special day. The street party in the picture would obviously need careful planning. Imagine one of the people in the picture was the main organiser and, a month before the event, had prepared a plan for the other organisers to discuss. Write down what you think he or she would write about each of the following:

decorations   food   activities for children
activities for adults   timetable for the day

Words

Mr. Truman told Paul he was receiving <u>red-carpet treatment</u>. This is an expression meaning he was a very special guest. It is taken from the idea that a red carpet is often laid down for very important people to step on.

Here are ten more interesting expressions including <u>red</u> or other colours. Write them down and explain what they mean, making sure you find out the meaning of those you do not know.

1	to see red	6	grey matter
2	once in a blue moon	7	to be caught red-handed
3	to have green fingers	8	a white lie
4	a white elephant	9	blue in the face
5	the black sheep of the family	10	a green belt

Language

In the last paragraph of the passage Etta told Paul about a letter that had arrived at her house. Imagine the letter had arrived in April 1980, and this was the letter and its envelope.

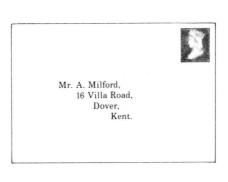

Maysted House,
Canterbury,
Kent.
16th April 1980

Mr. A. Milford,
16 Villa Road,
Dover.

Dear Mr. Milford,
    You will be pleased to know that Paul is very well and I should like to bring him to your house on 17th May. I hope this is convenient and look forward to hearing from you.
    I hope you, Mrs. Milford and Etta are all well.

Yours sincerely,
John Truman

Mr. A. Milford,
16 Villa Road,
Dover,
Kent.

A   Write a letter and an envelope from Mr. Milford to Mr. Truman to say the date is convenient. The examples above will help you with the layout.

B   Now write a letter and an envelope from Etta to Paul to say how pleased she is that he is coming. This letter should be much more chatty and contain news about what she has been doing.

The old wreck

The rusty old wreck lay in the mouth of the river, glistening with slimy seaweed. The wind howled through the holes in its sides. The little captain clambered up on to the lopsided deck and tried to find a way inside the ship. Podgy and Marinka crawled up after him. Rotted ropes and smashed chests lay all around.

"Hey!" cried Podge. "What does that say?"

Marinka bent over and tried to read the letters that sea and wind had almost wiped off one of the chests. "CIR," she read. "What does it mean?"

"It's the name of the ship, of course," said Podge.

But then the little captain called, "Come and help."

He had found a door, and all three of them put their shoulders to it and pushed. "One, two, three, hup!" They fell through it, and found themselves on a heap of canvas at the foot of some steps.

The darkness smelled stale and seemed full of little wriggly creatures. The floor was awash with water and in it squirmed crabs and jellyfish and shrimps.

"Funny. It smells like a stable," said Podge, puzzled.

"Watch out you don't get a stain on your new trousers," warned Marinka, grinning.

"Never mind that, just look." Podge pointed.

In the dim light they could make out that the cabin was divided into cubbyholes. Mouldy wooden partitions and boards still stood half upright.

"This must be where the pirates slept," said Marinka.

"Pirates?"

"Of course. With red beards and a patch over one eye. They each had to have a cubbyhole for their treasure."

"You're cracked," declared Podge.

"Suppose the pirates are on the island now?" cried Marinka. Her eyes sparkled. "Living at the back of the mountain. And they've caught Gus."

"Do you think that's it, captain?" asked Podgy, frowning.

But the little captain made no reply. He was looking around very thoughtfully. He had never seen such a strange ship.

"We must go and tell timid Thomas about the pirates," said Marinka. "He'll be pleased to hear that."

Thomas had stayed on the shore. Not for a whole sack of gold would he have climbed aboard an old wreck like that. He preferred to stay down on the sand and gaze at the wide sea and the foaming waves.

from 'The Little Captain' by Paul Biegel

Understanding

A   For each of the following write down **three** answers.

1   Evidence from the first paragraph that the ship was a wreck.
2   Evidence from the whole passage that the wreck had been there a long time.
3   Reasons the cabin the children fell into was worth exploring.
4   Things about the pirates Marinka imagined used to live on the ship.
5   Things about the ship that you think the little captain found strange.

B   Five children are mentioned in the passage: Podge, Marinka, Gus, Thomas and the little captain. Write down what you have learned from the passage about each of them.

My own work

A   Captains of ships keep a diary of what happens to the ship each day. This type of diary is called a log-book.

Imagine the ship in the passage really had been a pirate ship. Write a section from the captain's log-book about an adventure in search of treasure.

B   Now write another section from the log-book, describing how the ship came to be wrecked at the mouth of the river.

Perhaps the pirates in the picture are like the ones Marinka imagined had once sailed in the old wreck. Below are the names of five famous pirates. Find some information about each of them. Write a few notes about each one to show why he was famous. Give your work a suitable heading.

Long John Silver   Captain Kidd   Blackbeard
Sir Henry Morgan   Captain Hook

Words

A   Podge thought the name of the ship in the passage was CIR. In fact the full word on the chest had been CIRCUS and animals from a circus had travelled on the ship. The word had become a sort of abbreviation because CUS had been rubbed out.

Abbreviations are often used to shorten long words. Make a list of the following and opposite each one write the full word. Notice that an abbreviation is followed by a full stop.

Feb.	tel.	Yorks.	Co.	Ltd.
gym.	dept.	Prof.	Lib.	etc.

B   Most abbreviations use the first letter of each word. Write down each of the following and what it stands for.

B.B.C.	I.T.V.	H.M.S.	A.A.	G.M.T.
B.R.	m.p.h.	H.Q.	R.S.P.C.A.	O.H.M.S.

Language

A   The actual words spoken by someone in a story are called **direct speech** and are placed inside **inverted commas**.

Look at the direct speech in the passage. Notice that each time the speaker changes a new paragraph is started. The first word of a speech always has a capital letter. The speech ends with a comma if it is followed by <u>Podge said,</u> <u>said Marinka</u> etc., unless the speech is a question or an exclamation.

Write out five speeches from the passage to practise the correct punctuation.

B   Imagine Marinka and the others found Thomas and told him about the wreck. Write a few more lines of the story, including five pieces of direct speech, based on the following.

1   Marinka told Thomas excitedly they had explored the old wreck.
2   Thomas wanted to know more about it.
3   Marinka claimed there had been pirates on the ship and they were now on the island.
4   Podge interrupted to say Marinka was imagining things.
5   The little captain thought they would have to be very careful.

Danger from Red Indians

In the evening of a hot day early in July, Kit Carson, one of the mos
famous trappers of the time, came across a small emigrants' cam
between Fort Bridger and the Sublette Cutoff. Only one wagon wa
standing there; two horses and a number of cows were trying to find foo
between the stones and sagebrush.

Carson rode up at a gallop, leapt from his horse, and ordered a boy wh
came towards him to put out the fire.

It was a lad with hair bleached almost white by the sun and a face fu
of freckles. He was wearing a long red flannel shirt that came down to hi
knees. In his leather belt he had stuck two knives and a powder horn. Th
belt sagged crookedly round his narrow boy's hips with the weight of
heavy pistol in a holster. His eyes were bright and intelligent.

Without hesitation he did as Carson told him.

He ran to the wagon, brought out a spade, and threw earth over the fir
of buffalo droppings. Not until he had finished did he look up and asl
"Why do I have to do this?"

The strange man looked at him. Then he turned his eyes to the row c
children's faces staring from the wagon. It was late, and they ough
really to have been asleep. The big boy glanced round at them an
frowned. Then he laughed shyly, and said, awkwardly pointing:

"That's my brother and sisters."

"Oh, is that so?" said Carson, with a sick feeling in his stomach.

Those children were in danger. Indians were usually above killin
children, but the grown-ups who must surely also be there ran every ris
of being butchered. And if that happened, what would become of th
kids? And how in the world did this one wagon come to be standin
there, all on its own, in the middle of the wilderness?

"Why did I have to put out the fire?" John Sager asked again.

"Because there's a party of Sioux Indians on the warpath, that's why
They mustn't spy that smoke," Carson replied.

from 'Children on the Oregon Trail' by A. Rutgers van der Loe

Understanding

A   Using clues from the passage explain how you know each of the following.

1   There was something unusual about the wagon.
2   The boy (John Sager) was in charge of the wagon.
3   He did not know Kit Carson.
4   Kit Carson was in a hurry.
5   John Sager had spent a lot of time in the open air.
6   He was prepared for danger.
7   He had quick reactions.
8   The wagon was in a poor grazing area for cows and horses.
9   Indians were in the area.
10   The Indians were unlikely to be friendly.

B   Write down five pieces of evidence from the passage to show that it describes an incident in the United States.

My own work

A   Imagine Kit Carson and John Sager made a list of five plans they could use to try to save the wagon and the children from the Indians. Write out their list and for each plan explain its good points and any weaknesses you think it has.

B   Now write an exciting story showing how one of the plans you chose was used.

The wagon train in the picture was a common feature of the American West in the nineteenth century.

Below are ten more words linked to the American West. Find each word in a dictionary and write down the meaning. Give your list of definitions a suitable heading.

| prairie | wigwam | sheriff | ranch | squaw |
| buffalo | outlaw | tomahawk | canyon | stagecoach |

32

Sentences

In the first paragraph of the passage two types of people are named. A <u>trapper</u> is a person who traps animals usually in order to sell the fur. An <u>emigrant</u> is a person who leaves one place in order to settle in another.

For each of the following write a sentence that makes it clear what the person is or does. The first five words, like <u>trapper,</u> are concerned with work. The rest of the words, like <u>emigrant,</u> are connected with travel.

doctor	journalist	miner	newsagent	teacher
passenger	pedestrian	refugee	tourist	tramp

Language

A   **Apostrophes** are used to show **either** that a letter has been left out of a word **or** to show possession. Answer these questions about the apostrophes used in the passage.

1   Make a list of the words in which apostrophes are used.
2   Which words have apostrophes to show letters have been left out? How would the words have been written in full?
3   Which singular noun is followed by '<u>s</u> to show possession?
4   Which plural noun, ending in <u>s</u>. is followed by an apostrophe to show possession?
5   Which plural noun, **not** ending in <u>s</u>. is followed by '<u>s</u> to show possession?

B   Write out the following story, putting in the ten apostrophes that have been left out.

Kit Carson didnt have many enemies in Americas Far West. Usually he thought he was the Indians friend. Its true, however, that some of them couldnt accept Kit Carsons hand of friendship. He used to warn travellers about these Indians. "Keep together and theres much less risk," he told them, "and dont forget a fires easily seen from a long way." Even so, he often saw the fear in mens faces.

33

The woodpecker

Tread softly here,
The woodpecker's at work.
Don't disturb his ploy,
That long-billed boy
With his prod, prod, prod,
And jerk.

Somewhere in that beech,
Neither far nor near,
Out of sight, out of reach,
Seeking maggot and mite,
His divining rod
Makes its prod, prod, prod,
And jerk.

That tree must be hollow,
Or ear could not follow
The brittle bill
Taking its fill
After prod, prod, prod,
And jerk.

He earns his bite,
Sapping and tapping
From morning to night,
Mining the green
Where only the squirrel
And owl have been.

Let him work his will,
Don't disturb his ploy,
That quick-billed boy
With his prod, prod, prod,
And jerk.

Richard Church

Understanding

A
1. Where is the woodpecker?
2. What is the woodpecker doing?
3. Why is it easier to hear than to see the woodpecker?
4. Why do you think the squirrel and owl are mentioned in the poem?
5. What does the poet ask us not to do?

B
   From each verse choose one word or phrase that describes the woodpecker's beak at work. What does each word or phrase tell you about its beak?

My own work

   The poem describes the woodpecker's behaviour as it searches for food in the beech tree. Choose another bird or animal, either wild or a pet, that you have watched closely, read about or seen on television. Write a careful description of it and some of the things it does.

Bird-tables, like the one in the picture, help birds to survive the winter and allow us to watch them feeding. Below is a list of things you need to make a bird-table to hang from a branch. Use this to plan an **information sheet** showing how to make a bird-table. Make the information sheet attractive, giving it a pleasant design, with drawings if possible. Make sure the instructions are clear.

1 a piece of wood suitable for use outdoors
2 four pieces of wood to make edges for the four sides, so that the food will not fall off
3 screws or nails
4 nylon cord, to hang the bird-table from a branch

Spelling

Each of the following words (or pairs of words) from the poem is followed by a question about spelling. Check all your answers in a dictionary.

1 softly: **Adverbs** are usually formed by adding ly to an **adjective**. Write down the adverbs formed from these adjectives:
      brave   slow   faithful   usual   immediate
2 neither: This word is an exception to the rule i **before** e **except after** c. Write down three words that **keep** to the rule.
3 beech and reach: The spelling of words with this sound in the middle has to be learned. Write down five more words with the same sound and check them carefully.
4 taking and tapping: The long a sound means there is only one k in taking. The short a sound means there is a **double** p in tapping. Notice also that the e in take is left out of taking.
   Find three more words in the poem that end in ing and explain how each word follows the rules mentioned above.
5 brittle and squirrel: Most words with this sound end with le, but some that end in el have to be learned. Complete these words.
   litt . .   lev . .   tab . .   troub . .   quarr . .

Language

Here are summaries of information about three more birds. Use the information to write an interesting **paragraph** about each bird, putting the information in the order you think is best.

1 **robin:** 14 cm long – male and female alike – orange-red breast – young spotted – often very tame – lives in woods and gardens – eats worms, grubs, breadcrumbs – chosen as British national bird
2 **cuckoo:** usually grey – pointed wings and rounded tail – about 32 cm long – summer visitor to woods and moorland – winters in Africa – lays eggs in other birds' nests – young never know real parents – male makes 'cuckoo' call
3 **jackdaw:** 33 cm long – lives in flocks in towns, woods and farmland – nests on cliffs and churches and in big trees – black with grey head – bobs head when walking – call sounds like 'jack' – sometimes steals bright objects

unit 9

A Womble learns a lesson

It was a fine Spring dawn when Great Uncle Bulgaria set off to pay a call on Wellington. The old Womble sniffed the air with pleasure as he walked briskly across the grass, although he wrinkled his white nose in disgust as he crossed the Serpentine Road, for, with his still keen sense of smell, he was aware of a lingering whiff of exhaust fumes here. In all directions he could see silent bands of Wombles at work. Through the trees he caught a glimpse of Miss Adelaide with a line of very small Wombles trotting along behind her. She was teaching them the lay-out of the Park and showing them the best places to hide, should any Human Being suddenly appear. Tomsk was down by the Serpentine shovelling litter into his extra large tidy-bag, watched by an admiring ring of black-backed gulls, herring gulls, a kestrel, a great many mallards and even the lordly heron which was standing thoughtfully on one leg. Orinoco, who'd been having a nice forty winks, cosily tucked up in the hollow trunk of an old elm tree, hastily heaved himself out and began picking up crumpled newspapers and Bungo was trying to push an ancient garden roller up a slight slope.

Great Uncle Bulgaria paused, opened his mouth to call out and then closed it again. Young Bungo thought he knew the answer to everything, so it would do him no harm to learn a little lesson the hard way. Great Uncle Bulgaria leant on his stick and waited patiently and sure enough, Bungo, having reached the top of the small hill and obviously very pleased with himself, paused for a breather. He then discovered that what goes up, quite often goes down, and suddenly the roller began to trundle on its way, gathering speed as it did so.

A faint cry of "Oi – stop – oi" was wafted across the Park and the last view Great Uncle Bulgaria had of Bungo was of that young Womble hanging on desperately to the long handle of the roller, before he and it had both vanished over the brow of the bank.

from 'The Wombles at Work' by Elisabeth Beresford

Understanding

A   Five of the six Wombles named in the passage were busy. What was each of them doing? What other information about them have you learned from the passage?

B   Find each of the following in the passage. Explain what you think each of the underlined words means as it is used in the passage.

1   'he walked <u>briskly</u> across the grass'
2   'he <u>wrinkled</u> his white nose in disgust'
3   'a <u>lingering</u> whiff of exhaust fumes'
4   '<u>shovelling</u> litter into his extra large tidy-bag'
5   'an <u>admiring</u> ring of black-backed gulls'
6   'the <u>lordly</u> heron'
7   '<u>cosily</u> tucked up in the hollow trunk'
8   '<u>heaved</u> himself out'
9   'the roller began to <u>trundle</u> on its way'
10 'hanging on <u>desperately</u> to the long handle'

My own work

A   The book from which the passage is taken is called 'The Wombles at Work' and the passage shows the Wombles doing cleaning-up jobs in the Park. Imagine the Wombles visited your school during the night. Describe how they spent the night, the jobs they did and the fun they had as they tried to clean up.

B   Describe some of the ways you think your neighbourhood could be made cleaner and tidier.

Imagine you owned a shop that sold gardening goods, like the roller which Bungo could not control. Design an advertisement for a local newspaper and include in it some of the equipment you can see in the picture. Remember to include the name, address and telephone number of the shop. Use a newspaper or a mail-order catalogue to help you with ideas about the layout of advertisements and prices.

Punctuation

A   Here are three of the main ways commas are used in a story: to separate items in a list; to provide a pause in a long sentence; in pairs, like brackets, around extra information.

Look at the first paragraph of the passage, in which there are twelve commas, and explain why each comma is used.

B   Here are five sentences about the Wombles. The commas have been left out. Rewrite the sentences, putting in the commas that are needed. One of the sentences does not need any commas.

1   The day was warm dry and sunny.
2   The Serpentine Road normally very busy had very little traffic.
3   In the Park the Wombles were working hard.
4   Orinoco Bungo Tomsk and Miss Adelaide were there.
5   Orinoco who liked peace and quiet had found a place to rest.

Language

Nouns name things. Most nouns are **common nouns**, like <u>dawn</u> in the first sentence of the passage. Some nouns are **proper nouns** like <u>Wellington</u>. Proper nouns always begin with a capital letter.

There are two other types of noun. **Collective nouns** name groups of things, like <u>bands</u> in the third sentence of the passage. **Abstract nouns** do not name actual objects, but name things like feelings or ideas. An example of an abstract noun from the second sentence is <u>pleasure</u>.

1   Name three common nouns from the last paragraph of the passage.
2   Name three proper nouns from the whole passage.
3   Name another abstract noun from the second sentence.
4   Name a collective noun that might have been used instead of <u>bands</u> in the third sentence.
5   Name three more examples of each of the four types of noun. You may use words that are **not** in the passage.

A shock in the morning

On Friday morning, in the peaceful hour before the others were awake, Aunt Gwen leaned out of bed, boiled the electric kettle and made an early pot of tea. She poured out a cup for her husband, one for herself, and then she rose to take the third to Tom.

She was crossing the little hall with the tea, when she stopped dead, frozen at what she saw: the front door of the flat, which Alan himself had locked last night, was open. In a nightmare moment she saw them all in her imagination: robbers with skeleton keys, robbers with jemmies, robbers with sacks to carry away the swag; and each man wore a black mask and carried a deadly weapon – a bludgeon, a revolver, a dagger, a length of lead piping . . .

Gwen Kitson was recalled from her attackers by a painful sensation in her fingers: she was trembling so much that hot tea was slopping over the teacup into the saucer and scalding the hand that held it. She set the cup and saucer down on a hall chair, and, as she did so, she saw why the hall door remained open: it was wedged at the bottom by a pair of bedroom slippers – Tom's.

The imaginary burglars vanished. Tom must be responsible. She remembered that he had been found roaming out of bed one night when he had first come to stay with them. She remembered, too, the high words there had been then, with Alan, and she decided to manage this by herself.

First of all, she had a look outside on the landing: there was no sign of Tom. Then she removed the bedroom slippers, closed the door and went into Tom's bedroom. There he was, fast asleep – not even shamming, she was sure. She stood over him, the tell-tale slippers in her hand, wondering what she should say to him. She must scold him, and yet she did not want to be too hard on him and spoil his last day.

Even the mild reproach Aunt Gwen had prepared was never uttered. Tom, when she roused him, behaved in a way that too much alarmed her. He opened his eyes, but then at once squeezed them shut again, as if against a hateful sight. With his eyes closed, he began talking violently and in what seemed a senseless way: "No! Not this Time! Not Now!"

from 'Tom's Midnight Garden' by Philippa Pearce

Understanding

A   A good title for the first paragraph would be 'An Early Morning Cup of Tea'. Give each of the other paragraphs a suitable title. The six titles should then be a summary of the whole passage.

B   What do you think Aunt Gwen felt when each of the following happened?
1   She saw the front door open.
2   She saw the bedroom slippers wedged in the hall door.
3   She realised Tom must have been out.
4   She saw Tom was fast asleep.
5   She saw that Tom was having a bad dream.

My own work

A   Aunt Gwen was daydreaming about burglars in the house. Imagine you had a dream about burglars in **your** house. Describe what happened in your dream.

B   Tom had been dreaming about something that frightened him. Describe some of the things that occur in dreams that might have frightened Tom.

The picture and passage give impressions of two very different types of homes at night or in the early morning. Below is a list of ten types of buildings in which people live. Write out the list and for each building write down a **definition**, without looking at a dictionary.

palace	cottage	flat	hotel	tent
shack	bungalow	mansion	igloo	penthouse

Now compare your definitions with those in a dictionary.

44

Spelling

The endings of words need special care. Here are some examples.

1 Some words end in <u>ful</u>, like <u>beautiful.</u> Find three more in the passage.
2 Some words end in <u>ly</u>, like <u>deadly</u> in the second paragraph. What words ending in <u>ly</u> are formed from <u>complete</u>, <u>faithful</u>, <u>sincere</u>?
3 Some words end in <u>tion</u>, like <u>sensation</u> in the third paragraph. Form words ending in <u>tion</u> from <u>create</u>, <u>collect</u>, <u>operate</u>.
4 Words ending in <u>ary</u>, <u>ery</u>, <u>ory</u> have to be learned, like the word <u>imaginary</u> in the fourth paragraph. What word ending in <u>ary</u> is the name of a book in which you find the meaning of words? What word ending in <u>ery</u> is the name of a place where monks live? What word ending in <u>ory</u> is used to describe events that happened in the past?
5 Some words end in <u>able</u> and some in <u>ible</u>. Add the correct ending to the following. The first word is in the fourth paragraph of the passage.

respons _____   sens _____   comfort _____
remark _____   horr _____

Language

A   Each of the following is a way of stressing a word, a sentence or an idea. Find one example of each in the passage.

> an exclamation mark
> a dash
> a row of dots
> a word repeated three times in two lines
> the first letter of a word spelt with a capital letter
>   that was not really needed

B   Now look at the first sentence of the second paragraph of the passage. Choose one word that you think should be stressed and rewrite that part of the sentence five times, using each of the following methods of stressing the word.

> capital letters   underlining   thick writing
>   inverted commas   italics

The frightening house

The darkness was thinning. Soon the road ran across a stretch of heath on which, still some way ahead of them, a dark mass stood out against the gradually lightening sky. After a few moments, Pongo saw that the dark mass was a great stone wall.

"There you are," said the cat. "Your puppies are behind that."

"It looks like the wall of a prison," said Pongo.

"*Nasty* place," said the cat. "The Colonel will tell you its history."

She led them from the road over the rough grass of the heath. As they drew nearer, Pongo saw that the wall curved – as the wall of a round tower curves. Above it rose the trunks of tall trees, their bare branches black against the sky.

"You'd think there would be a castle, at least, inside that huge wall," said the cat. "And they do say there was going to be, only something went wrong. All that's there now – well, you can see for yourself."

She led the way to the rusty iron gates, and Pongo and Missis peered through the bars. There was now enough light for them to see some distance. Beyond a stretch of grass as wild as the surrounding heath they saw the glint of water – but, strangely, it seemed to be *black* water. Then they saw the reason why. Reflected in it was a *black* house.

It was the most frightening house Pongo and Missis had ever seen. Many of the windows in its large, flat face had been bricked up and those that were left looked like eyes and a nose, with the front door for a mouth. Only there were too many eyes, and the nose and the mouth were not quite in the right places, so that the whole face looked distorted.

"It's seen us!" gasped Missis – and it really did seem as if the eyes of the house were staring at them from its cracked and peeling black face.

"Well, that's Hell Hall for you," said the cat.

She moved on and they followed her, round the curving wall. After a few minutes they saw a tower rising high above the tree-tops. It was built of rough grey stone, like the wall, and was rather like a church tower. But there was no church. The tower simply jutted out of the wall. Some of the narrow windows were broken and their stonework was crumbling. The place was not yet a ruin but looked as if it quite soon might be one.

from 'The Hundred and One Dalmatians' by Dodie Smith

Understanding

A   Explain what you think each of the following means.

   1   'the darkness was thinning'
   2   'the road ran across a stretch of heath'
   3   'their bare branches black against the sky'
   4   'the whole face looked distorted'
   5   'their stonework was crumbling'

B   When Pongo saw each of the following, what do you think were the main impressions he got?

   1   the wall
   2   the gates
   3   the water
   4   the house
   5   the tower

My own work

A   Imagine the Colonel told Pongo some stories about what had happened long ago in the black house described in the passage. Tell one of the stories in the way you think the Colonel would tell it.

B   Describe in detail an old building you have seen.

The picture shows a knight arriving at a castle, perhaps like the one mentioned in the passage, that was planned but never built. Here are ten words that name parts of a medieval castle. Use a dictionary or encyclopaedia to find the meaning of any you do not know.

moat	portcullis	keep	walls	bailey (inner)
drawbridge	gatehouse	battlement	towers	bailey (outer)

Draw a plan of a castle, labelling it with the words in the list. Check your plan by looking at a book on castles in the library.

Spelling

A   Find the following words in the passage.

against   lightening   quite   staring   rising

Each of these words may be confused with the following words that have different **meanings** and **pronunciations**.

again   lightning   quiet   starring   raising

Explain the differences between the five pairs of words.

B   The following story contains ten pairs of words that might be confused. Rewrite the story, choosing the correct word from each pair.

The children had chosen a difficult **rout/route**. They had managed to **lose/loose** the way but at last they **were/where** at the camp and could **bath/bathe** their feet and put on clean **cloths/clothes**. One **affect/effect** of the heat was that there was hardly a **breath/breathe** of air. All the children were very **tired/tried accept/except** Brian who still had the energy to write about the day in his **dairy/diary**.

Language

A   Most **verbs** are **action** words, like <u>moved</u> at the beginning of the last paragraph of the passage. A few verbs, like <u>was</u> in the first sentence, describe a **state** not an action. Sometimes verbs consist of more than one word, like <u>had been</u>.

Make a list of the verbs in the first four paragraphs of the passage.

B   Verbs may be in the **present**, the **past** or the **future** tense.

1   Write down the tense of each of the verbs you listed in Part A.
2   The description of the tower in the last paragraph of the passage is in the **past tense**. Rewrite it in the **present tense**.
3   Write a short, exciting paragraph in the **past tense** to describe Pongo and Missis creeping up to Hell Hall. Now rewrite the same paragraph in the **present tense**. Which paragraph do you think makes the adventure seem more exciting?

Hide and seek

Call out. Call loud: "I'm ready! Come and find me!"
The sacks in the toolshed smell like the seaside.
They'll never find you in this salty dark,
But be careful that your feet aren't sticking out.
Wiser not to risk another shout.
The floor is cold. They'll probably be searching
The bushes near the swing. Whatever happens
You mustn't sneeze when they come prowling in.
And here they are, whispering at the door;
You've never heard them sound so hushed before.
Don't breathe. Don't move. Stay dumb. Hide in your
    blindness.
They're moving closer, someone stumbles, mutters;
Their words and laughter scuffle, and they're gone.
But don't come out just yet; they'll try the lane
And then the greenhouse and back here again.
They must be thinking that you're very clever;
Getting more puzzled as they search all over.
It seems a long time since they went away.
Your legs are stiff; the cold bites through your coat;
The dark damp smell of sand moves in your throat.
It's time to let them know that you're the winner.
Push off the sacks. Uncurl and stretch. That's better!
Out of the shed and call them: "I've won!
Here I am! Come and own up I've caught you!"
The darkening garden watches. Nothing stirs.
The bushes hold their breath; the sun is gone.
Yes, here you are. But where are they who sought you?

Vernon Scannell

Understanding

A   The poem tells you what the author was doing or thinking about as his friends tried to find him. Write down five things he **did** to stop them finding him.

B   Now write down five things he **thought** about while he was hiding.

My own work

A   Imagine you were playing hide and seek around your house and were looking for good hiding places either inside or outside the house. Choose what you think would be the five best places, describe them and say why you think each of them would be suitable.

B   Hide and seek is a game often played in school playgrounds. Describe some of the other games that are played in your school playground.

We do not know the names of the children mentioned in the poem or those shown in the picture. Choose ten of the children in the picture and give each of them a first name. Now, with the help of your teacher, find a book that gives the meanings of people's first names. Make a list of the meanings of the names you have chosen.

You may also wish to find the meanings of the names of other people you know, including your own!

Sentences

The poem contains sentences of different lengths, including some good examples of very short sentences to add excitement or tension to the story.

Here is the outline of a story for you to write out in full. As you are writing it, use sentences of a suitable length and think of good links between your sentences.

1 summer evening – very hot
2 playing fields – children playing hide and seek and other games
3 loud noise of aeroplane
4 one child first to recognise helicopter – flying very low
5 children very excited – some frightened
6 helicopter pilot signals children to keep clear
7 helicopter lands on playing fields – police arrive
8 ambulance arrives – takes injured climber from helicopter to nearby hospital
9 children thanked by police – helicopter takes off
10 children run home to tell parents

Language

A   **Pronouns** replace nouns and are usually used to avoid repeating a noun unnecessarily. The most common pronouns are

I me he she it him her we us you they them.

Which of these pronouns are used in the poem?

Which pronouns did you use in your story about the helicopter?

B   Sometimes pronouns are used carelessly and the meaning is not clear. Explain why the meaning of each of the following sentences is not clear and rewrite it to avoid the **ambiguity**.

1 Jane's mother told her to keep away from Amanda as she had a cold.
2 The girls went out to look for their dogs. Have you seen them?
3 They wanted their parents to wake up early but when they got up next morning they were still asleep.
4 Jane told Amanda that she would have to make breakfast.
5 It seemed to Jane that every time she opened her mouth she put her foot in it.

The search in the wood

"I don't want to," Sammy said.

"Cowardy custard." But Prue was uncertain herself. They stood on the path and looked through the broken fence into Turner's Wood. A few shafts of sunlight filtered down through the trees, but it was mostly dark dark green and secret.

Sammy said, "Suppose he's there? Suppose he jumps out?"

"He won't. He didn't before. He only turned nasty when we teased him."

Sammy still hung back. Prue said, "Don't you want to find Squib?"

Sammy sighed, very deeply.

Prue jerked his arm. "It was you said he lived there, you said he told you. Was that a *lie*?"

Sammy shook his head.

"Cross your heart?"

He licked his forefinger and drew it across his throat. His eyes were big. He said, "Suppose the witch catches us and puts *us* in the basket and fattens us up to eat?"

"*That's* not true. Not the witch part." But Prue hesitated. She might not listen to most people, but she listened to Sammy. Though he was smaller and weaker in every other way, his imagination was stronger; his tales became true in the telling. And the wood did look very dark.

Sammy said fearfully, "It's a chanted wood. A chanted wood round a castle."

"*En*chanted, silly. And it's not a castle, just the Old People's Home." Prue felt suddenly bolder. She said, "Oh, come on . . ."

Sammy had no choice: she held him by the wrist. Through the fence and into the wood – quite a long way into it, in her first, determined rush. He stumbled after her, through tangly undergrowth that plucked his clothes and scratched his ankles. He thought he saw dark shapes out of the corners of his eyes. He said, "Prue . . ." and sobbed in his throat.

She stopped so abruptly that he bumped into her. She said sternly, "All right then, go back. Go back by yourself."

He pressed closer. "I heard something." They listened. There were small sounds all round them; leaves rustling, twigs cracking. The wood was alive . . . "Squirrels," Prue said. "Birds," and, as if to answer her, a pigeon bubbled up aloft.

"There you are," she said.

from 'Squib' by Nina Bawden

Understanding

A   What have you learned from the passage about each of the following?

1   the wood
2   Prue
3   Sammy
4   why the children were in the wood
5   the Old People's Home

B   Write down five words or phrases the author uses to make the wood seem frightening.

My own work

A   The passage mentions someone or something called Squib that the children were looking for. Write a description of Squib, as you imagine him or it to be.

B   Now imagine Squib appeared in the wood. Write the next part of the story, describing what happened when the children met Squib.

Perhaps the Old People's Home in the picture is like the one mentioned in the passage. The two nurses clearly are enjoying their job of looking after elderly people. Here is a list of ten other people whose occupations involve service to the public. For each one write a few notes, describing the work that person does.

teacher	doctor	librarian	councillor
ambulanceman	journalist	magistrate	dentist
policeman or policewoman		postman or postwoman	

Words

In the passage Sammy confused the words <u>chanted</u> and <u>enchanted</u>. Here are the meanings of ten words beginning with the letters <u>en</u>. For each one write down the correct word. The first one is done for you.

1 under the effect of a spell: <u>en</u>chanted
2 a door through which you go into a building
3 an opponent in war
4 huge
5 a paper cover used to enclose a letter
6 to go into a place
7 a book giving information on all subjects
8 to take pleasure in something
9 a person who performs on stage or on television or in films
10 to help or give confidence to someone

Language

A   **Adjectives** are **describing words**. They describe nouns or pronouns. Answer these questions about the adjectives used in the passage.

1 Write down three adjectives used to describe the wood in the second paragraph.
2 Choose a good synonym that means the same as <u>nasty</u> in Prue's second speech.
3 Write down the three comparative adjectives used to compare Prue and Sammy in the paragraph beginning, "That's not true."
4 Which adjective did Sammy mispronounce?
5 Near the end of the passage an unusual adjective is used to describe the undergrowth. What is it and what do you think it means?

B   Interesting adjectives are an important part of good writing. Choose an interesting adjective to describe each of the following.

1 an old woman
2 a bowl of fruit
3 a story you have read
4 a stream
5 your last holiday
6 a soldier
7 a flower bed
8 a cave
9 one of your neighbours
10 a tiger

Changing colours

When the sun got up the next morning, Thatch had already placed hi
ladder against Fooley Hall and climbed up on the roof to start work
With his bundle of dried reeds on his back, he crawled along, whistling
softly around the clove of garlic he always sucked as a remedy agains
chills, and counting in his head the number of gold pieces he would have
by the end of the week.

When he reached the chimney, he stood up to survey the roofs still to
be done in the new scalloped fringe – one gold-bit for each. It was an
encouraging sight, and Thatch's heart swelled with happiness. Roofs to
the north of him, roofs to the west of him, roofs to the . . . Perplexed
Thatch turned back to scan the houses on the west side of the marke
place. What was different about them this morning? What – ? He clutched
the chimney in astonishment.

Curley Green's door was as green as the greenest door on the square

"Well!" said Thatch, shifting the garlic from one cheek to the other. He
swept his gaze round the market place, at the rows of shining white
houses and uniform green doors. Then he clutched the chimney again
his eyes almost popping out of his head. Across the square from Curley
Green's door glowed a splotch of bright colour. Thatch blinked and
blinked again. It was Muggles's house, and her door was painted a vivid
orange!

"Well!" said Thatch, and gaped so broadly that his garlic fell out and
rolled down the roof unheeded.

Other folk had more to say when they discovered the changes wrough
during the night. Small groups clustered together on the cobbles to
whisper and glance sidelong at the two doors, broke up, and reclustered to
whisper some more. Somebody – no one knew who – started a rumour
going that Geo. the Official Village Painter knew more about Curley
Green's painted door than Curley Green herself. When this news
circulated itself among the clusters, there was a sound like a gobble o
fish snapping at green flies.

Reedy, the basketmaker's wife, was indignant. "Right or wrong," said
she, "it's Curley Green's door, and Geo. has no business meddling with i
behind her back."

from 'The Minnipins' by Carol Kendal

Understanding

1 What work do you think Thatch was going to do on the roof of Fooley Hall?
2 How does the first paragraph suggest Thatch was a hard-working man?
3 How did he intend to spend the rest of the week?
4 Why did his heart swell with happiness?
5 When Thatch looked round the market place what colour did he expect almost all the doors to be painted?
6 Why was he surprised at the colour of Curley Green's door?
7 What other surprise did he have?
8 What happened to show that Thatch was **very** surprised?
9 How did the rest of the villagers react to the changes?
10 Why was Reedy so angry with Geo?

My own work

A Imagine you could improve the outside appearance of the buildings where you live. What changes would you make?

B Now write a story, describing the reactions of your family and neighbours if the changes you wanted to make actually happened one night.

The picture shows the centre of a small town or village, very different from the old village described in the passage. Imagine the street in the picture included ten more buildings as well as the newsagent and the hotel. Make a plan of the street, showing the other buildings and what they are used for. Try to include a suitable range of buildings, such as shops, a bank and a post office.

Now, for each building that would have one, design a name-plate like the two in the picture.

Spelling

A These five words all occur in the passage.

   already   different   happiness   shining   business

They are all common words that are often mis-spelt. Find each one in the passage and write it out carefully.

B Now write the heading 'Common words that are often mis-spelt'. Write down the five words from Part A and add to the list these fifteen words, learning the spelling of each as you write it down.

beautiful	believe	people	occasionally	separate
immediately	favourite	receive	surprise	disappear
mysterious	beginning	definite	useful	excitement

Add to your list five more words you know how to spell but which you think are difficult. Now make sure you can spell **all** twenty-five words in your list.

Language

Near the end of the passage, the sound of the villagers' gossip is compared to fish snapping at flies. This type of comparison is called a **simile**.

Imagine you were the writer of the passage and had to choose similes for each of the following. What would you choose?

1 Thatch as he worked on the roof
2 the taste of his garlic
3 the roofs all around him
4 the colour of Curley Green's door
5 the colour of Muggles's door
6 Thatch's eyes as he saw the changes
7 Thatch's mouth as he opened it in surprise
8 the garlic as it rolled down the roof
9 the villagers as they gathered together
10 Reedy as she got angry

61

An exciting time

'Jingle Bells' was playing for the second time as Chris crept up th
stairs to the staffroom. There were extra presents on the table becaus
sometimes extra brothers and sisters came to the party. They wer
already wrapped in red paper and Chris felt them carefully. Two ba
point pens, red and blue, would be nice for Liberty, and the nurse
uniform with the red cross on the hat for Pattella, and the little doll i
the bed for Minta. A car drew up and Chris looked out of the windov
Father Christmas was getting out. Chris scribbled the names in black fe
pen and ran down and put them on top of the other presents, just a
Father Christmas came into the hall.

He had a scarlet robe and a white beard and big black boots, and h
said, "Ho, ho, ho. Are there any good children here?"

The Infants squealed and went bright pink, and Dickie was bouncin
up and down like a jumping bean. Class Six smiled but nobody squealec
and Linda whispered, "Funny thing that. Father Christmas has got
watch like Mr. Page's."

"Hush," said Miss Lee. "You don't want to spoil it for the little ones.

"Ho, ho, ho," said Father Christmas a few more times, and then h
went over to the Christmas tree and picked up the top present.

"Liberty Lovell," he read out and looked a bit surprised.

"Go on," whispered Chris, and Liberty got up in his cowboy hat an
walked to Father Christmas; his sisters went with him.

"Liberty Lovell, are you a good boy?" Father Christmas said, bu
Liberty said nothing. "Ah well . . . nice to have you with us," Fathe
Christmas said, and patted the top of Liberty's hat. Then he gav
presents to each of the little girls.

"Fancy them getting presents; they only come to school two days,
said Mary.

"Not fair," said Tom, as the Lovells came back to their places.

"Linda Jones," said Father Christmas. "Ho, ho, are you a good gir
Linda Jones?"

"Don't open your presents now, please children," Miss Lee said, bu
the Lovells were already tearing at their red paper. Liberty looked at h
pens and grinned. After that everybody opened their presents as fast a
they got them. There was red paper everywhere, and Father Christma
left out the bit about being a good boy or girl and just called the name
and gave out the presents as fast as he could.

from 'Nowhere to Stop' by Geraldine Kay

Understanding

A   Explain **why** you think each of the following happened. In some cases a word is in **bold** type to help you with your answer.

1 'Jingle Bells' was playing for the **second** time.
2 The extra presents were **already** wrapped in red paper.
3 Chris put the extra presents on **top** of the others.
4 Class Six smiled but did not squeal like the Infants.
5 Linda was puzzled about Father Christmas's watch.
6 Father Christmas looked surprised when he read Liberty Lovell's name.
7 Liberty's sisters went with him to get his present.
8 Mary and Tom were not happy about the Lovells' presents.
9 Miss Lee did not want the children to open the presents straight away.
10 Father Christmas gave out the presents as **fast** as he could.

B   What were the main things you learned about each of the following?

1 Father Christmas
2 Chris
3 the Lovells
4 Miss Lee
5 the school

My own work

A   Imagine you could choose exciting Christmas presents for five people you know well. Describe the present you would choose for each person, explaining why you made that choice.

B   Father Christmas is often to be found giving presents to small children in big department stores. Imagine you were Father Christmas for one hectic hour in a store just before Christmas. Describe what happened.

Both the passage and the picture make you think of Christmas and, especially, the date we remember best, 25th December. Here are ten more dates that are very important.

1st January	14th February	29th February	15th March	1st April
23rd April	21st June	31st October	5th November	11th November

Make a list of the dates and write down information about each one to show why it is important. For some of them you may need to use a suitable reference book.

Now use a calendar to note the day of the week of each date **this** year. Watch out for one date that may be difficult to find!

Spelling

A   Find each of the following words in the passage, write them down and note that each of them is spelt as **one** word, not two.

already   everywhere   nobody   sometimes   everybody

B   Now here is a list of ten more words that are each spelt as **one** word, not two. Write ten sentences about Christmas, using a different word from the list in each sentence.

another	meanwhile	nowhere	today	anybody
itself	somebody	downstairs	outside	tomorrow

Language

A   In the passage Father Christmas seemed to like to ask each child the same question, "Are you a good boy?" or "Are you a good girl?"

Make up five questions that you think a small child might want to ask Father Christmas.

B   The two questions written out in Part A show that a question mark, if it is needed, always comes **inside** inverted commas.

Imagine a conversation between Mary and Tom, two children mentioned in the passage. Mary is asking Tom some riddles. Here is the beginning of the conversation. Continue it to include four more riddles that you know, making sure you use correct punctuation, including inverted commas and question marks.

Mary asked Tom, "Why do Swiss cows wear bells?"

"I know that one," said Tom. "It's because their horns don't work."

A message on the rock

The children stood for some minutes, held by the splendour of the view. Then Susan, noticing something closer to hand, said, "Look here! This must be one of the mines."

Almost at their feet a narrow trench sloped into the rock.

"Come on," said Colin, "there's no harm in going down a little way – just as far as the daylight reaches."

Gingerly they walked down the trench, and were rather disappointed to find that it ended in a small cave, shaped roughly like a discus, and full of cold, damp air. There were no tunnels or shafts: the only thing of note was a round hole in the roof, about a yard across, which was blocked by an oblong stone.

"Huh!" said Colin. "There's nothing dangerous about *this*, anyway."

All through the afternoon Colin and Susan roamed up and down the wooded hillside and along the valleys of the Edge, sometimes going where only the tall beech stood, and in such places all was still. On the ground lay dead leaves, nothing more: no grass or bracken grew; winter seemed to linger there among the grey, green beeches. When the children came out of such a wood it was like coming into a garden from a musty cellar.

In their wanderings they saw many caves and openings in the hill, but they never explored farther than the limits of daylight.

Just as they were about to turn for home after a climb from the foot of the Edge, the children came upon a stone trough into which water was dripping from an overhanging cliff, and high in the rock was carved the face of a bearded man, and underneath was engraved:

DRINK OF THIS
AND TAKE THY FILL
FOR THE WATER FALLS
BY THE WIZHARDS WILL

"The wizard again!" said Susan. "We really must find out from Gowther what all this is about. Let's go straight home now and ask him. It's probably nearly tea-time anyway."

from 'The Weirdstone of Brisingamen' by Alan Garner

Understanding

A   Imagine Susan and Colin were telling Gowther about their afternoon's adventures. What would they tell him about each of the following? Use only the information in the passage.

          1   the Edge
          2   the cave
          3   the beech woods
          4   the stone trough
          5   the carving in the rock

B   The children said they would ask Gowther some questions when they went home. Write down five questions you think they would ask him about what they had seen during the afternoon.

My own work

A   Choose one of the questions you wrote in Part B of **Understanding**. Write a conversation between Gowther and the children during which the question is discussed and answered.

B   Imagine the children returned to one of the caves mentioned in the passage, this time with a torch. Write a story about the adventure they had.

Rocks and cliffs, like those described in the passage and shown in the picture, are usually found on the coast. Below are the names of ten places in Britain which are near interesting cliffs or coastlines. Use an atlas to help you draw an outline of the British Isles. Now find each of the places in the atlas and write the names of the places accurately on **your** map.

Dover	Torquay	Land's End	Cardigan	Llandudno
Isle of Skye	John o'Groats	Holy Island	Bridlington	Cromer

Handwriting

A   Write out the saying that was carved on the rock, using your best handwriting.

B   Each of the following is a well-known saying because it is the opening of a famous poem. Write out each one neatly.

1   'Oh, to be in England
Now that April's there.'

2   'He clasps the crag with crooked hands,'

3   'Season of mists and mellow fruitfulness,'

4   '"Is there anybody there?" said the Traveller,'

5   'Tiger! Tiger! burning bright
In the forests of the night,'

Language

A   Here is a list of **prepositions**, the short words that usually introduce phrases:

for   by   into   at   in   of   from   along   after   among

Find an example of each of them in the passage and write down the phrase it introduces.

B   Below are five prepositions **not** used in the passage. Write five sentences about Colin and Susan. Each sentence should start with a phrase that begins with one of the prepositions.

near   with   above   behind   .during

unit 17

The rabbits face danger

As the sun sank lower and touched the edge of the cloudbelt on the horizon, Hazel came out from under the branches and looked carefully round the lower slope. Then he stared upwards over the ant-hills, to the open down rising above. Fiver and Acorn followed him out and fell to nibbling at a patch of sainfoin. It was new to them, but they did not need to be told that it was good and it raised their spirits. Hazel turned back and joined them among the big, rosy-veined, magenta flower-spikes.

"Fiver," he said, "let me get this right. You want us to climb up this place, however far it is, and find shelter on the top. Is that it?"

"Yes, Hazel."

"But the top must be very high. I can't even see it from here. It'll be open and cold."

"Not in the ground: and the soil's so light that we shall be able to scratch some shelter easily when we find the right place."

Hazel considered again. "It's getting started that bothers me. Here we are, all tired out. I'm sure it's dangerous to stay here. We've nowhere to run to. We don't know the country and we can't get underground. But it seems out of the question for everybody to climb up there tonight. We should be even less safe."

"We shall be forced to dig, shan't we?" said Acorn. "This place is almost as open as that heather we crossed, and the trees won't hide us from anything hunting on four feet."

"It would have been the same any time we came," said Fiver.

"I'm not saying anything against it, Fiver," replied Acorn, "but we need holes. It's a bad place not to be able to get underground."

"Before everyone goes up to the top," said Hazel, "we ought to find out what it's like. I'm going up myself to have a look round. I'll be as quick as I can and you'll have to hope for the best until I get back. You can rest and feed anyway."

"You're not going alone," said Fiver firmly.

from 'Watership Down' by Richard Adams

Understanding

A   Explain how the **first** paragraph gives you information about each of the following.

1 the time of day
2 where the rabbits were
3 whether or not they had been there before
4 their feelings about their situation
5 their behaviour

B   Now use the rest of the passage to answer these questions.

1 Why did the rabbits feel it would be dangerous to stay at the bottom of the hill?
2 Why did they feel it would be safer at the top?
3 What were the problems about climbing the hill?
4 What do you think Hazel would look for when he climbed to the top of the hill?
5 How do you know that the three rabbits were the leaders of a much larger group?

My own work

A   The rabbits of 'Watership Down' had to make a long journey full of danger. Imagine that, as part of their journey, they had to pass through the area where you live (or another area you know well). Write a story about this part of the journey and how they overcame the problems they faced.

B   Everything in the story is seen through the eyes of the rabbits. Choose a much smaller creature, like an ant or a mouse, and describe its world as you think it sees it.

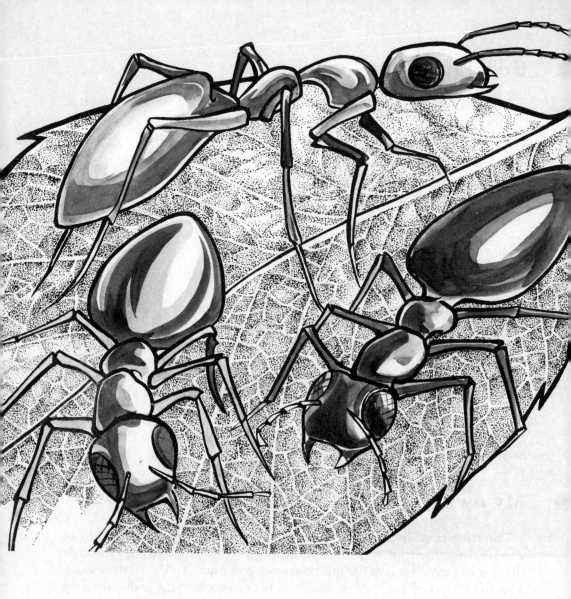

The ants in the picture may be similar to those that made the ant-hills that Hazel and the rabbits saw. Use encyclopaedias or books on insects to find information about ants. As you are reading, make notes about such things as their size, appearance, food, breeding and, especially, habits and behaviour which are often very unusual and interesting.

Now set out the information you have noted to make an interesting and attractive **information sheet** about ants.

Sentences

A   Look at the paragraph in the passage beginning, 'Hazel considered again'. Notice that, to show Hazel's anxiety, the sentences he spoke are all very short.

Write a similar paragraph, with about eight short sentences, in which Hazel reported to the other rabbits what he had seen at the top of the hill.

B   Descriptions usually have longer sentences and include more adjectives. Write a descriptive paragraph of two or three sentences about the area the rabbits would find at the top of the hill.

Language

A   **Adverbs** give you more information about the verbs they describe. Like adjectives they help to make writing more effective and interesting.

Look at <u>carefully</u> in the first sentence of the passage. It tells you **how** Hazel looked around. Write out the last part of the sentence **without** the word <u>carefully</u>. You can see how much less information you have.

Choose five adverbs that might have been used in the sentence but which would have added very different information, for example <u>quickly</u> or <u>happily</u>. Write out the last part of the sentence five times, each time with one of **your** adverbs and notice how the choice of adverbs is very important.

B   Here is a passage about Hazel and the rabbits. Write it out, choosing an interesting and effective adverb for each of the ten spaces.

Hazel, Fiver and Acorn _____ made their plans. They _____ collected together the other rabbits and told them _____ about the situation. Darkness fell and one by one the rabbits set off _____ up the hill. Almost all the rabbits had _____ reached the top when _____ there was a high-pitched scream from below. Hazel ran _____ down the hill but it was too late! One of the rabbits must have been caught by a fox and _____ it was never seen again. That night the remaining rabbits slept _____ in their new burrows and there they stayed _____ until they were fit for the next stage of their journey.

All along the street

The stopping, starting traffic
And the tipper-tap of feet
Weave a tapestry of magic
All along the street.

Summer awnings striped with rainbows
Drop blocks of shadows on the street,
Shadow slashed with cuts of sunshine,
Shadow sliced with knives of heat.
All is mine, and without paying;
Not one penny do they charge
For all this treasure,
And they throw in for good measure
The stopping, starting traffic
And the tipper-tap of feet
That weave a tapestry of magic
All along the street.

A band comes, fills the street
With throbbing music hammered out of drums,
With shining music kept in time to marching feet.
And then I pass a flower-stand,
Where roses sparkle, roses blaze
Pink and yellow, – deepest red.
There is no command to buy this pleasure;
So, at my leisure
I stand and gaze.
Here a rich, brown smell of coffee,
There a bakery smell of bread;
Not for sale, but given free;
And they throw in for good measure
The stopping, starting traffic
And the tipper-tap of feet
That weave a tapestry of magic
All along the street.

F. J. Teskey

Understanding

A 1 Why is the title of the poem such a suitable one?
2 Write down two things that appeal to the poet's sense of sight.
3 Write down two things that appeal to the poet's sense of hearing.
4 Write down two things that appeal to the poet's sense of smell.
5 What does the poet feel about paying for all the pleasure he is having?

B What thoughts do you think were going through the poet's mind when he chose each of the following phrases?

1 'the tipper-tap of feet'
2 'summer awnings striped with rainbows'
3 'shadow slashed with cuts of sunshine'
4 'shadow sliced with knives of heat'
5 'shining music'

My own work

A The poem describes a shopping street on a busy day in summer. Think of a shopping street or shopping centre you know well. Write a description of the place, the shops, shopkeepers and shoppers, the traffic etc. on a busy Saturday. Try to involve the senses in the same way that the poet did.

B Now describe the same place on the following Sunday morning when there is hardly anyone about.

The buses in the picture remind you of the 'stopping, starting traffic' in the poem. One of the buses has an **indicator** that shows the number of the bus and the main places it passes through on its **route**. Choose three bus routes you know and make an indicator for each one, like the one in the picture.

Now choose one of the three routes and make a map to show the route the bus takes from one terminus to the other.

Words

A   The traffic in the poem is described as <u>stopping, starting.</u> These two words are opposite in meaning. Here are five more words ending in <u>ing</u> that could have been used to describe the traffic. For each one choose another word ending in <u>ing</u> that is opposite in meaning.

beginning   arriving   slowing   moving   filling

B   Words opposite in meaning are called **antonyms**. Here are ten adjectives that might be used to describe a shop or shopping area. Choose an antonym for each.

noisy	busy	modern	boring	friendly
clean	ugly	cheap	cramped	elegant

Language

The first four lines of the poem form a complete sentence. Each of the lines on its own would **not** form a sentence. It is the idea of **completeness** that a sentence needs and it is important to understand this and know where a sentence ends.

Write a good complete sentence about each of the following, using the descriptions and information in the poem.

the traffic
the feet
the street
the shadows
the band
the drums
the flower-stand
the coffee
the bread
the weather

A changed house

A thin, elderly man stood before them holding a candlestick aloft. He wore a heavy, dark-red dressing-gown and on his head was a white stocking cap with a tassel which fell to his shoulder.

"I beg your pardon," said the Professor.

"How can I help you, sir?" said the elderly man.

"Why I—is—is this the house of Professor Euclid Bullfinch?" asked the Professor.

"Alas, no," said the man. "The house is mine. There is no Professor here, neither Bullfinch nor other."

"I see." The Professor cleared his throat. "Well, is this the town of Midston?"

"Yes, this is Middestown. But I know of no Professor Bullfinch here." He glanced past the Professor at the four huddled young people.

"However, I fear the late hour has sent my courtesy to the winds, sir," he continued. "It is clear to me that you are lost, and here I keep you and your children standing on the doorstone. Please come in, the night air is chill and you must be a-weary."

The Professor hesitated. Then he said, "You're very kind, sir. Come on, kids."

They entered the house, and Danny stared about in astonishment. It was the same house and yet there were differences which leaped out at him even by the uncertain candlelight. The hall seemed smaller, somehow, until he realized that the familiar wallpaper with its bright design of wreaths was gone. Instead the walls were painted a rather drab tan. The stairway was plain, dark wood instead of being white. The stranger led them into the parlour to the left, and here, although the fireplace with its heavy beam and mantelpiece, and the small-paned windows, and the wide floor boards were all as he remembered them, the furnishing had mysteriously changed. Gone were the comfortable over-stuffed armchairs, the couch, the bookshelves, and the television set. Instead, there were three or four straight chairs, a heavy pine table, and two rather stiff-looking wooden armchairs. A few books in thick leather bindings lay on the table, and there were candles in tin sconces fastened to the walls. Here, too, the wallpaper had vanished; there was plain wooden panelling on the fireplace wall, and the other walls were smooth plaster. There was no rug on the floor, and the room seemed rather chilly and bare.

from 'Danny Dunn-Time Traveller' by Jay Williams & Ray Abrashkin

Understanding

A   1   Write down two things from the first paragraph that help to show that the Professor and the children had gone back two hundred years into the past.

       2   Write down two words or phrases the elderly man used that he would be unlikely to use today.

       3   What is interesting about the name of the town?

       4   What do you think was the main change Danny noticed in the hall of the house?

       5   What do you think was the main change he noticed in the parlour?

B   Make two columns. At the top of the first column put this year's date. At the top of the other column put the date of the year two hundred years ago. Now make lists showing the differences Danny found when they travelled back in time two hundred years.

My own work

A   The last paragraph of the passage describes the Professor's house as it was two hundred years ago. Imagine the Professor and the children returned to our time, bringing the elderly man with them. Write another paragraph describing their return and the elderly man's reactions to what he saw.

B   The last four sentences of the passage describe in detail the appearance of the parlour. Look around the room you are now in and write a careful description of its appearance and what it contains.

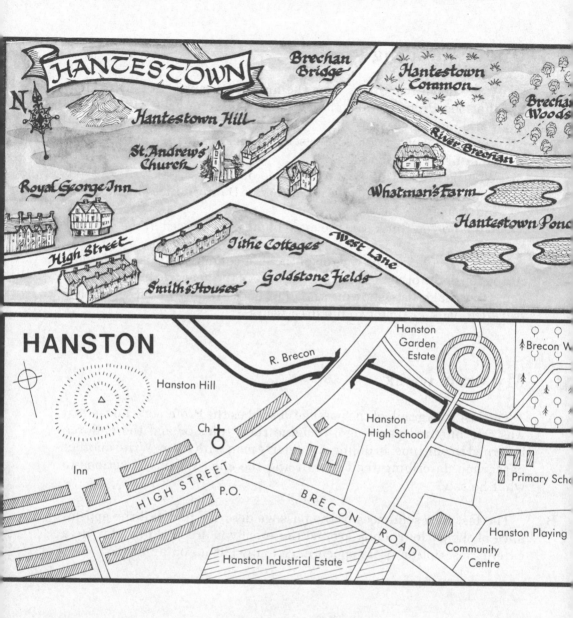

The two maps give an idea of the way a town like the one mentioned in the passage changed during the last two hundred years. Look **closely** at the two maps and make three lists, one of things that have stayed almost the same, one of things that have changed quite a lot, and one of things that are new.

Punctuation

A   In the passage two types of **proper nouns** can be found: the name of a town, Midston, and the names of a person, Professor Euclid Bullfinch. Proper nouns always begin with a capital letter.

Write down the names of ten towns and ten famous people.

B   All the following types of proper nouns also begin with a capital letter. For each one write down three examples.

1   days of the week
2   months of the year
3   names of countries
4   names of streets
5   names of the planets
6   names of schools
7   names of famous buildings
8   titles of books
9   names of battles
10 makes of cars

Language

A   Look at the two nouns <u>candlestick</u> and <u>dressing-gown</u> in the first paragraph of the passage. These are called **compound nouns** because they are formed by joining two nouns to make a single noun. Compound nouns **may** be spelt with a **hyphen** (candle-stick). <u>Dressing-gown</u> has a hyphen to separate the two letters <u>g</u> in the middle of the word.

Write down five more compound nouns from the last paragraph of the passage.

B   Below are ten nouns. Add another noun to each one to form a compound noun. The first one is done for you.

rain – rainbow	book	
foot	mouse	
light	road	
house	sea	
sun	water	

81

When the bull arrived

The children set down the heavy blackberry baskets and the thick jerseys the twins had long since discarded, pulled off shoes and stockings, and splashed across to where a small group of trees formed a miniature wood, cool and inviting. Here, on the exposed roots of a big willow, they sat for a while, their feet in the stream, dabbling their hands in it and every now and then splashing their hot faces with the cool clear water. Presently a wood-pigeon, cooing plaintively behind them, attracted their attention and they turned away from the stream and crept quietly in among the trees, trying to catch a glimpse of it until, startled by something, with a frightened cry and a loud flutter of wings, it flew off. When they turned back to the stream once more, cows were strolling by on the opposite bank and one, more inquisitive than the rest, was investigating the jerseys and the blackberry baskets.

"Cows!" exclaimed Jim who was a little in front of the others.

"Cows won't hurt you!" said Kate with the scorn born of nearly six weeks of country life.

"That's not a cow, you sillies!" said John sharply from behind her. "It's a *bull*!"

It was undoubtedly a bull, though not a very large one. It had knocked over one of the baskets now and the grass was strewn with blackberries. As they approached, it moved nearer the bank, then nearer still, finally taking up a stand with its forefeet planted firmly on John's blue jersey, regarding them with a fixed, unblinking stare. Would it suddenly charge – dash into the stream, up the bank and into the trees after them . . ? It looked very much as if it might . . . Kate was frightened. Cows were safe enough; a bull was quite another matter . . . "Always respect a bull," Mr. Digweed had impressed on her more than once; "it's only a fool that doesn't," and Mr. Digweed *knew*.

"Quick!" she cried to the twins. "*Quick!* Climb up this tree. It can't reach us there!" The next minute the three of them were wriggling and squirming their way among the branches of a large willow. The bull, however, remained where it was – staring stonily. And it continued to do so.

from 'Holiday at the Dew Drop Inn' by Eve Garnett

Understanding

Answer **yes** or **no** to each of the following questions and in each case explain how the passage helped you to decide on each answer.

1   Were the children on a walk in the countryside?
2   Was it a hot day?
3   Did the children cross the stream in order to find the wood-pigeon?
4   Was the pigeon frightened by the children?
5   Did the children live in the countryside?
6   Had the cows been following the children?
7   Were the cows on the same side of the stream as the children?
8   Were the children frightened by the bull?
9   Was the bull behaving dangerously?
10   Did the children run away?

My own work

A   Continue the story, describing what happened next to the children when they were in the willow tree, with the bull staring at them from across the stream.

B   Now write another adventure about Kate and the twins in which they learnt another lesson about the countryside.

The bull in the picture looks fiercer than the one described in the passage, and the notice on the gate is needed! Here are five more notices you might see in the country. For each one make a notice that is clear and would attract interest.

PLEASE SHUT THE GATE   PICNIC AREA
PUBLIC FOOTPATH   ANCIENT MONUMENT
TRESPASSERS WILL BE PROSECUTED

Now design five more notices that you might see in a **town**, either on the street or in a park.

Spelling

A   Some words contain letters that are not sounded. Find an example in the passage of each of the following and add another word of your own that follows the same rule.

1   a word with an unsounded <u>b</u>
2   a word with <u>gh</u> not sounded
3   a word beginning with an unsounded <u>w</u>
4   a word beginning with an unsounded <u>k</u>
5   a word including <u>ia</u>, in which only one of the two letters is sounded.

B   Answer these questions on some more types of unusual spelling and pronunciation. You may find a dictionary helpful.

1   Some words end in <u>ough</u> (cough). Write down three more words with the same ending but each with a different pronunciation.
2   Some words begin with an unsounded <u>h</u> (honour). Which **three** of these words begin with an unsounded <u>h</u>?
          hour   hotel   human   heir   honest
3   Some words begin with <u>pn</u> or <u>ps</u> in which the <u>p</u> is not sounded (psalm). Write down three more words beginning with an unsounded <u>p</u>.
4   Sometimes <u>qu</u> has a <u>kw</u> sound, as in <u>question</u>. Sometimes it has a <u>k</u> sound, as in <u>opaque</u>. Write down one more example of each sound.
5   Some words are pronounced very differently from the way they are spelt. Use a dictionary to find out how each of the following is pronounced: colonel   aisle   yacht   lieutenant   viscount.

Language

1   Look at the next to the last paragraph of the passage. Each of the first two sentences includes a **conjunction** which joins together the two parts of the sentence. Write down the two conjunctions.
2   Which of the following conjunctions are also used in the passage to join parts of sentences together?
    when   but   until   although   before   while   as   because
3   Look at the sentence later in the paragraph, 'Kate was frightened.' Suppose the author had given a reason using the conjunction <u>because</u>. What do you think she would have written?
4   Now write five sentences beginning 'Kate was frightened', followed in each case by a different conjunction and a suitable ending.
5   It is unusual (but not wrong) to begin a sentence with <u>And</u> when you want to make the sentence especially exciting or emphatic. Which sentence does the author of the passage use in this way?

The tramp in the park

Henry decided to go to the park, and for the first time ventured outsid
into the street. All the gates were closed, the curtains neatly drawn back
He saw the milkman, and that was all.

The park was deserted. He wandered gloomily through the wrough
iron gates and made for the aviary, where he glowered ferociously at th
golden-eyed tropical birds. Picking up a stick he ran it noisily over th
bars of their cages. They flew in a rainbow whirl of feathers, squawkin
their protest. The cockatoos bristled and threw out angry ruffs.

Henry sauntered off towards the swings. He passed a gardener puttin
in bedding plants.

"Good morning," he said.

"Morning." The man did not even lift his head. He knelt hunchbacke
over his boxes, deaf and self-contained as a tortoise.

Henry went right to the farthest side of the park, where narrow path
twisted among the shrubbery. He had given up hope. And then h
rounded a sudden corner, looked up, and saw the tramp. Sun struck th
dew that glinted on his hair and beard. Wild, wicked and impossible, h
loomed among the clipped, self-respecting laurels.

"Good gracious!" said Henry.

"Good morning," said the tramp. "Nice day. Lovely. *Glorious*."

"Very nice," agreed Henry, delighted to be in conversation wit
someone at last, especially with a tramp of whom his mother woul
certainly have disapproved. He was folding newspapers with hi
mittened fingers.

"Making me bed," he explained. "Least, packing it up. Can't let thi
lot go. Nothing like 'The Times' for warmth, and not so easy to come by
every day of the week."

"You've been sleeping rolled up in newspapers!" said Henry, en
chanted. "Are they really warm?"

"Downright frost-proof," said the tramp. "Though sacks is good. Fai
to middling, sacks."

He had finished stacking his newspapers and put them into the woode
handbarrow parked by the seat.

"Seen any keepers?" he inquired.

"Only a gardener," said Henry, "and I think he was deaf. Don't they le
you sleep here, then?"

"Not if they can help it," the tramp replied, "but they can't help it, mostly. I just nip among the bushes till they shut the big gates for the night. Worst thing is if they find you in the morning, first thing. Nasty shock that. Very nasty. I don't go in much for park sleeping."

from 'The Night Watchmen' by Helen Cresswell

Understanding

A   What have you learnt from the passage about each of the following?

1 the tramp's appearance
2 the way he spent the nights
3 his attitude to the life he led
4 his attitude towards parks and park-keepers
5 Henry's attitude towards the tramp

B   What is the most interesting information you learned about each of the following?

1 Henry
2 Henry's mother
3 the park
4 the gardener in the park
5 the aviary

My own work

A   In the passage Henry changed from being very bored to becoming very excited when he met the tramp. Describe a day you remember when something happened that made your mood change completely.

B   The other main character in the passage is the tramp. Imagine the park-keeper came along and the tramp had to leave the park quickly. Describe what happened to him during the rest of that day.

The tramp in the picture is about sixty years old. Try to imagine the main events of his life, including what made him become a tramp. Now make a **time-chart** of the whole of the tramp's life. Include in your time-chart the dates of five very important events in the world as well as in the tramp's life.

Punctuation

When Henry saw the tramp he said, "Good gracious!" The **exclamation mark** is used to stress Henry's surprise. Exclamation marks are also used to show anger, fear and other strong emotions.

Write down what you think Henry would say in each of the following situations. Each answer should need an exclamation mark.

1 The tramp offered him a bite of his sandwich.
2 The tramp asked him if he'd like to become a tramp.
3 He suddenly saw the park-keeper approaching.
4 The tramp told him he was really a rich man.
5 His mother asked him if he'd had an interesting day.

Language

A In Units 6 and 16 you were asked to write out conversations, using **inverted commas** correctly. The last part of the passage about Henry and the tramp is mainly conversation. Imagine Henry asked the tramp three more questions about his life, and the tramp answered each question. Write out the conversation that would be added to the passage.

B Another use of inverted commas is for titles, for example 'The Times', the newspaper the tramp used to keep him warm. Write out the following, using capital letters and inverted commas correctly.

1 the names of five newspapers, magazines or comics
2 the titles of five books
3 the titles of five songs
4 the names of five television programmes
5 the titles of five passages in this book

My father

Some fathers work at the office, others work at the store;
Some operate great cranes and build up skyscrapers galore;
Some work in canning factories counting green peas into cans;
Some drive all night in huge and thundering removal vans.

But mine has the strangest job of the lot.
My father's the Chief Inspector of – What?
O don't tell the mice, don't tell the moles,
My father's the Chief Inspector of HOLES.

It's work of the highest importance because you never know
What's in a hole, what fearful thing is creeping from below.
Perhaps it's a hole to the ocean and will soon gush water in tons,
Or maybe it leads to a vast cave full of gold and skeletons.

Though a hole might seem to have nothing but dirt in
Somebody's simply got to make certain.
Caves in the mountain, clefts in the wall,
My father has to inspect them all.

That crack in the road looks harmless. My father knows it's not.
The world may be breaking into two and starting at that spot.
Or maybe the world is a great egg, and we live on the shell,
And it's just beginning to split and hatch: you simply cannot tell.

If you see a crack, run to the phone, run!
My father will know just what's to be done.
A rumbling hole, a silent hole,
My father will soon have it under control.

Keeping a check on all these holes he hurries from morning to night.
There might be sounds of marching in one, or an eye shining bright.
A tentacle came groping from a hole that belonged to a mouse,
A floor collapsed and Chinamen swarmed up into the house.

A hole's an unpredictable thing –
Nobody knows what a hole might bring.
Caves in the mountain, clefts in the wall,
My father has to inspect them all!

Ted Hughes

Understanding

A How does each of the following help to make this poem humorous?

1 the name, <u>Chief Inspector of HOLES</u>
2 the third line of the second verse
3 the hole to the ocean (third verse)
4 the <u>harmless</u> crack in the road (fifth verse)
5 the hole that belonged to a mouse (seventh verse)

B
1 Why do you think the poet begins by describing so many **other** jobs?
2 Why do you think the last word of the second verse is written in capital letters?
3 Write down three nouns from the poem, all beginning with <u>c</u>, which name different types of hole.
4 The poet says his father's work is 'the strangest job of the lot' and 'work of the highest importance'. Do you think the poem has made you agree with each of these statements?
5 If you could choose another title for the poem, what would it be?

My own work

A Write down the names of ten adults you know and the name of the job each one does. Now choose **five** of the jobs that seem to you to be interesting. Find out more about them, and write a description of each of the five jobs.

B If you could choose any job you would like to do when you grow up what would it be? Why would you choose that job in particular?

The poet's father might have to inspect the deep hole made by the excavator in the picture! The people watching the work seem to be observing very closely. Imagine you were testing how accurate their observation was. Make up five questions about the picture that you would ask someone who had just been watching the work.

Words

A In question B 3 of **Understanding** you had to find three types of hole mentioned in the poem. Use a dictionary to help you explain what type of hole each of the following is.

gap	groove	ravine	tunnel	slit
cavern	gully	chink	trench	chasm

B Imagine the poet had used five of the words above at the end of different lines of the poem and needed a suitable rhyme for each word. Choose words that would fit the idea of the poem.

Language

A Look at the word <u>unpredictable</u> in the last verse of the poem. The **root** of the word is <u>predict</u>. The **prefix** <u>un</u> changes the meaning and the **suffix** <u>able</u> makes the verb into an adjective.

Here are five more words consisting of prefix, root and suffix. Write down the root of each word, and explain how the prefix and suffix add to the meaning of the root.

transcontinental   semi-detached   disobediently
rearrangement   indigestible

B Here are five more prefixes with their meanings, and examples. Write down another word beginning with each prefix.

tele = from a distance (telephone)
sub = under   (submerge)
anti = against   (antiseptic)
post = after   (postscript)
mono = single   (monocle)

A ride with an unusual relative

The children gazed at their great-aunt, so startled by her appearance that the polite greetings they would have made vanished from their minds. Naomi was so scared that, though tears went on rolling down her cheeks, she did not make any more noise. Great-Aunt Dymphna had turned her attention to the luggage.

"Clutter, clutter! I could never abide clutter. What have you got in all this?" As she said 'this' a rubber boot kicked at the nearest suitcase.

"Clothes mostly," said Alex.

"Mummy didn't know what we'd need," Penny explained, "so she said we'd have to bring everything."

"Well, as it's here we must take it home, I suppose," said Great-Aunt Dymphna. "Bring it to the car," and she turned and, like a great black eagle, swept out.

Both at London airport and when they had arrived at Cork a porter had helped with the luggage. But now there was no porter in sight and it was clear Great-Aunt Dymphna did not expect that one would be used. Alex took charge.

"You and Naomi carry those two small cases," he said to Robin. "If you could manage one of the big ones, Penny, I can take both mine and then I'll come back for the rest."

Afterwards the children could never remember much about the drive to Reenmore. Great-Aunt Dymphna, in a terrifyingly erratic way, drove the car. It was a large incredibly old black Austin. As the children lurched and bounced along – Robin in front, the other three in the back – Great-Aunt Dymphna shot out information about what they met in passing.

"Never trust cows when there's a human with them. Plenty of sense when on their own. Nearly hit that one but only because that stupid man directed the poor beast the wrong way."

As they flashed past farms dogs ran out barking, prepared at risk of their lives to run beside the car.

"Never alter course for a dog," Great-Aunt Dymphna shouted, "just tell him where you are going. It's all he wants." Then, to the dog: "We are going to Reenmore, dear." Her system worked for at once the dog stopped barking and quietly ran back home.

For other cars or for bicycles she had no respect at all.

from 'The Growing Summer' by Noel Streatfeild

Understanding

A Answer each of the following questions about Great-Aunt Dymphna.

1 What did the children think of her when they first saw her?
2 How did she describe the luggage?
3 What did she do to the nearest suitcase?
4 What help did she offer to move the luggage?
5 How did she look as she went out?
6 How did she drive the car?
7 How did she talk in the car?
8 What was her attitude towards the cow and the man they passed?
9 How did she treat the dog they passed?
10 How did she treat the other road-users?

B Now write a description of Great-Aunt Dymphna's appearance and behaviour, using the information you collected in Part A.

My own work

A Write a description of any interesting adult you know well, in the same way that you wrote the description of Great-Aunt Dymphna. As well as describing the person's appearance and behaviour, make your account more interesting by including one or two stories about the person.

B The passage mentions the suitcases the children had with them. Imagine you were going to stay with an aunt for a week. What would you put in **your** suitcase?

Great-Aunt Dymphna could be just as kind as the elderly lady comforting the sick child in the picture. Most children have had to stay in bed for a while to recover from the usual childhood illnesses. Find information about each of the following illnesses to help you complete a **table**, showing the name of the illness, the symptoms, and the way the illness is usually treated.

measles   chicken pox   mumps   German measles   tonsilliti

Punctuation

Here are ten questions about the punctuation used in the passage.

1 How many sentences are there in the first paragraph?
2 Why are **two** commas used in the second sentence?
3 Write out Great-Aunt Dymphna's first speech, making sure the punctuation is correct.
4 Why is there an exclamation mark at the end of the first sentence of this speech?
5 What does the third sentence of her speech tell you about the placing of question marks?
6 Why are there inverted commas around the word this in the last sentence of the same paragraph?
7 Write down three words in the passage that include an apostrophe to show one or more letters have been left out.
8 Write down the names of three places mentioned in the passage.
9 Look at the sentence, 'It was a large incredibly old black Austin'. Some authors would have included commas in this sentence. Where do you think they might be put?
10 In the last sentence of the same paragraph the author includes two dashes. What other punctuation mark could she have used?

Language

A   One paragraph in the passage begins with the **adverb** Afterwards. Adverbs that change the time are very useful in stories but care must be taken to avoid beginning too many sentences with Then and Next.

Here are five good adverbs of time. Use each one to begin a sentence about the children's stay with Great-Aunt Dymphna.

soon   later   once   frequently   sometimes

B   A phrase to show a change of time is a useful way to begin a new paragraph. For example, later in the story a paragraph might begin 'Early next morning'. Write down five more phrases of time to begin paragraphs later in the story.

Search for treasure

Tolly spent the morning being a detective looking for hidden jewels. He went round the house tapping the walls to see if there were hollow places in the stone, especially at the back of cupboards, and looking at the floorboards to see if there were boards that had been cut short and screwed back again. It was a good game, but he did not find anything. Orlando went with him, a keen assistant who was always in the way, always first, always underneath him, blowing down cracks and barking whenever a cupboard door was not opened quickly enough.

Tolly asked his great-grandmother if he could look in her room, and she said yes, if he left everything as he found it. Orlando ran ahead up the stairs and when Tolly followed him into Mrs. Oldknow's bedroom he caught him at his tricks again, wagging at someone who wasn't there, but if someone had been there he or she would seem to be sitting in child's armchair that Mrs. Oldknow kept there. In this room there were window-seats in the recesses under the big windows, with cushions on the seats and a wooden front below them making a box which sounded hollow when tapped. Tolly looked in the wooden panel for signs of a door which might have lost its knob, or perhaps a drawer which would pull out, but the front was solid. He pulled off the cushion and examined the seat. Orlando stood on his hind legs and blew in rhythmic puffs under the ledge. Sure enough, it was a lid, but it had not been opened for so long that Tolly could not move it. However, at last, as he heaved with all his might, it came up with a protesting squawk. Inside was a large linen bag full of bits and pieces that were now familiar to him from the patchwork, a doll's patchwork quilt made to scale, a battered wooden doll that Orlando seized and went off with, shaking it like a rat and lovingly chewing it like a bone. Tolly should perhaps have stopped him, but he had found a small wooden ship, apparently hand carved, very elaborate, with a long bowsprit and three masts. The name 'Woodpecker' was painted on the bows. It was an unexpected shape, low in the bows and high in the stern, but not at all clumsy like a galleon. He felt its lines, weighed it in his hands, and knew that it would ride the water well. He took a great fancy to it, and longed to ask Mrs. Oldknow if he could keep it.

from 'The Chimneys of Green Knowe' by Lucy M. Boston

Understanding

A   Each of the following might be the answer to a question about the passage. In each case make up a suitable question to fit the answer.

1   a detective
2   the floorboards
3   Tolly's great-grandmother
4   Mrs. Oldknow's bedroom
5   window seats
6   the wooden panel
7   a lid
8   a battered wooden doll
9   a small wooden ship
10   'Woodpecker'

B   Orlando was exploring the house with Tolly. Make a list of five mischievous things the dog did.

My own work

A   Like Tolly, everyone dreams of finding treasure. Write a story with the title, 'The day I found the treasure chest in the garden'.

B   Many stories and films have been about hidden treasure. Think of one you have read or seen or heard about and tell the story as you remember it.

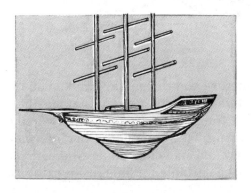

Both the picture and the passage make you think of treasure and the excitement of finding a great hoard that may have been buried for many years. Perhaps the greatest treasure discovered this century was that of the Egyptian king, Tutankhamun. Find information about this treasure from the library and encyclopaedias. Make an interesting booklet about it, that might be suitable for sale at an exhibition of the treasure.

Spelling

A   Some basic rules about spelling need to be learned and five very important ones are listed below. Find one example in the passage of each rule. To help you, an example **not** in the passage is given in each case.

1 Words like <u>al</u>ready begin with <u>al</u> **not** <u>all</u>.
2 Words like <u>anybody</u> and <u>somewhere</u> are spelt as one word **not** two.
3 Adverbs like <u>sincerely</u> are formed by adding <u>ly</u> **not** <u>ley</u> to the adjective.
4 A **double** consonant usually follows a **short** vowel, for example <u>bitten</u> **not** <u>biten</u>.
5 Most verbs that end in <u>e</u> lose the <u>e</u> when <u>ing</u> is added, for example <u>writing</u> **not** <u>writeing</u>.

B   Now think of three more examples to fit each of the following five important rules.

1 Words like <u>beautiful</u> end with <u>ful</u> **not** <u>full</u>.
2 Most words like <u>receive</u> and <u>believe</u> follow the rule **i before e except after c**.
3 Words ending in a **consonant** and **y** form their plural by removing the <u>y</u> and adding <u>ies</u> (lorry – lorries).
4 Words ending in a **vowel** and **y** form their plural by just adding <u>s</u> (donkey – donkeys).
5 Words beginning <u>**ex**</u> and an **s sound** need a <u>c</u> after <u>ex</u> (ex<u>c</u>ellent). Words beginning <u>**ex**</u> and a **z sound** have neither <u>c</u> nor <u>s</u> after <u>ex</u> (example).

Language

Look at these two sentences: The name of the ship was 'Woodpecker'. This was painted on the bows.

Write down three different ways of joining these two sentences to form one sentence. Now find the sentence in the passage and see if you have included the way the author chose, which was probably the best way of all.

The May fair

"It's here!" yelled George across the yard one fine Saturday morning
"It's never!" shouted back Val. "Cor, George, let's go over there at
once. When did it come?"

"Must've been last night. There wasn't anything yesterday."

For days the boys had been watching for the May fair that came every
year to the Common. The may trees were covered with a thick foam of
creamy blossom and their leaves were fresh and brilliant. It was high
time for the fair to arrive.

Like magic cities, it had grown up in a night. The great long travelling
wagons, and the lorries that carried the bumper cars, switch-backs and
horses were arranged in a huge circle on the fairground. A spring wind
was blowing dust in everybody's eyes, but the work went as smooth
routine, the show people assembling the booths and machines as if they
were mechanical toys. All the boys from the streets round the Common
were there, watching, messing about and getting in the way.

Soon the electricity was linked up, and by evening the whole place
leapt into a brilliant riot of noise and light. Thousands of bulbs of
different colours sparkled and glittered, outlining the booths; raucous
music from electric organs was broadcast from every corner, the
different tunes shouting each other down or being split asunder by the
screaming sirens of the flying boats.

At the back of the show, in the green dusk, the show people had set up
their usual domestic lives, strung their washing to the may trees, and
filled their dustbins with rubbish. The babies and dogs played beneath
the wagon wheels, while old crones peeled potatoes and stoked the
stoves that puffed blue smoke out of the wagon chimneys.

The boys had saved all their pennies for the fair, and each evening they
tried to decide between delicious hot dogs that were bedded down in fried
onion, or candy floss, pink, synthetic and amusing to eat. It cost a lot of
money to ride on the horses or go down the helter-skelter tower, and even
more to shoot with rifles at the dancing ping-pong balls. There were great
crowds round the shooting booths, but it was a shilling to have a go with
one of the rifles that never threw true.

from 'Magnolia Buildings' by Elizabeth Stucley

Understanding

A   What have you learned from the passage about each of the following?

1   where the boys lived
2   the time of year when the fair came
3   how often it visited the area
4   what sort of fair it was
5   how the fair was set up
6   how the fairground was made exciting
7   which of the sideshows attracted most people
8   what the boys did while the fair was being set up
9   what the boys did at the fair
10   where the show people lived

B   Write down one way each of the five senses (sight, hearing, taste, smell and touch) is involved in the passage.

My own work

A   Imagine you went to the fair one evening with George and Val. Write a story about your visit.

B   One of the most exciting features of many fairgrounds is the Ghost Train. Imagine you had the opportunity to design a Ghost Train for the fairground in the passage. Describe your Ghost Train and what it would contain.

The gipsy caravan in the picture might have been seen at a fair many years ago. Like many words, <u>gipsy</u> and <u>caravan</u> have interesting histories and a good dictionary will tell you something about the **derivation** or origin of each word. For example, <u>caravan</u> is from a Persian word naming a group of people who travelled together for safety.

Here are ten more words linked to the picture or passage. Find each word in a good dictionary and make a list of their derivations. Sometimes the derivation is not known!

gipsy	camp	family	pony	smoke
fair	May	lorry	rifle	ping-pong

Words

A   The author of the passage chose many lively and interesting words.
Write down the words she used to show or describe each of the following.

1   George's excitement (a verb)
2   the blossom (an adjective)
3   the leaves (two adjectives)
4   the noise and light of the fairground (a noun)
5   the brightness of the bulbs (two verbs)
6   the noise of the music (an adjective)
7   the noise of the sirens (an adjective)
8   the hot dogs (an adjective)
9   the candy floss (three adjectives)
10   the ping-pong balls (an adjective)

B   Now choose ten lively and interesting words for the gaps in the
following story about the fairground. Write out the story and underline
the words you have chosen.

The next morning George and Val _____ to the fairground. Everything was _____. Some of the show people were _____ the litter and
_____ it into _____ paper sacks. Others were _____ the sideshows and
making sure they were _____ for the next night. George and Val felt very
_____. They knew that the _____ fair had still one more _____ evening
before it left.

Language

In Unit 24, and also in Unit 3, there were questions about the way good
sentences can be built up. Five good sentences from the passage are
described below. Write down the first and last words of each of them, and
explain why you think they are good sentences.

1   a sentence that sets the scene on the Common before the fair arrived
2   a sentence that describes the way the vehicles that carried the fair
    were arranged
3   a sentence that lists the activities of the local boys
4   a sentence that lists the activities of the show people behind the
    fairground
5   a sentence that links the boys' money with the interesting food they
    could buy

Encounter with a wolf

Miyax stared hard at the regal black wolf, hoping to catch his eye. She must somehow tell him that she was starving and ask him for food. This could be done she knew, for her father, an Eskimo hunter, had done so. One year he had camped near a wolf den while on a hunt. When a month had passed and her father had seen no game, he told the leader of the wolves that he was hungry and needed food. The next night the wolf called him from far away and her father went to him and found a freshly killed caribou. Unfortunately, Miyax's father never explained to her how he had told the wolf of his needs. And not long afterwards he paddled his kayak into the Bering Sea to hunt for seal, and he never returned.

She had been watching the wolves for two days, trying to discern which of their sounds and movements expressed goodwill and friendship. Most animals had such signals. The little Arctic ground squirrels flicked their tails sideways to notify others of their kind that they were friendly. By imitating this signal with her forefinger, Miyax had lured many a squirrel to her hand. If she could discover such a gesture for the wolves she would be able to make friends with them and share their food, like a bird or a fox.

Propped on her elbows with her chin in her fists, she stared at the black wolf, trying to catch his eye. She had chosen him because he was much larger than the others, and because he walked like her father, Kapugen, with his head high and his chest out. The black wolf also possessed wisdom, she had observed. The pack looked to him when the wind carried strange scents or the birds cried nervously. If he was alarmed, they were alarmed. If he was calm, they were calm.

Long minutes passed, and the black wolf did not look at her. He had ignored her since she first came upon them, two sleeps ago. True, she moved slowly and quietly, so as not to alarm him; yet she did wish he would see the kindness in her eyes. Many animals could tell the difference between hostile hunters and friendly people by merely looking at them. But the big black wolf would not even glance her way.

from 'Julie of the Wolves' by Jean Craighead George

Understanding

A   Make a list of all the information you can find in the passage about each of the following.

    1   the black wolf
    2   Miyax's problems
    3   how Miyax was trying to solve her problems
    4   Miyax's father
    5   the animals of the Arctic

B   Now choose **one** of your lists and write an interesting paragraph using the information you included in the list.

My own work

A   Miyax was lost, without food, in the Arctic. Imagine you were going to spend some time in an isolated place. What preparations would you make and what would you take with you?

B   In the first paragraph of the passage there is a story about Miyax's father and some wolves he encountered. A short tale of this sort, included in a longer story, is called an **anecdote**. Anecdotes usually begin with a phrase like 'I remember once' or 'One day'.

    Write an anecdote about yourself, or someone else you know, that you could have included in Part A of this question.

The picture shows six Arctic animals like the ones Miyax would have seen during her adventures. The picture is like those you see in Field Guides, books that help you to identify wild animals, birds, trees and flowers. Opposite the pictures there is information about the size, colour, habits, etc. of each animal or bird.

Make a page for a Field Guide to be placed opposite the picture above. Use reference books to find information about the animals, which are: **a** walrus, **b** polar bear, **c** fox, **d** hare, **e** reindeer and **f** wolf.

Words

At the end of the third paragraph of the passage two adjectives are used to describe opposite moods of the black wolf. The adjectives are <u>calm</u> and <u>alarmed</u>. In the last paragraph two very different types of people are described by the words <u>friendly</u> and <u>hostile</u>.

Here are two lists of adjectives. Each list is in alphabetical order. For each word from the first list find an **antonym** in the second list, a word that has the opposite meaning.

brave	conceited
cautious	cowardly
cheerful	drowsy
confident	guilty
gentle	miserable
innocent	noisy
lively	reckless
modest	savage
quiet	stupid
sensible	uncertain

Language

A   The first sentence of a paragraph should be interesting and also introduce the main idea or **topic** of the paragraph.

Write down the topic of each paragraph in the passage. Explain how the first sentence of each paragraph helps to introduce the topic. Notice that two of the paragraphs begin with similar sentences but have different topics.

Now give each paragraph a suitable title to fit the topic.

B   Imagine these titles were chosen for five more paragraphs from the story 'Julie of the Wolves'. Write a good opening sentence for each paragraph.

1   The wolves come nearer
2   Confidence grows
3   Noises in the night
4   A speck on the horizon
5   Food at last

Friendly voices

Bilbo had escaped the goblins, but he did not know where he was. He had lost hood, cloak, food, pony, his buttons, and his friends. He wandered on and on, till the sun began to sink westwards – *behind the mountains*. Their shadows fell across Bilbo's path, and he looked back. Then he looked forward and could see before him only ridges and slopes falling towards lowlands and plains glimpsed occasionally between the trees.

"Good heavens!" he exclaimed. "I seem to have got right to the other side of the Misty Mountains, right to the edge of the Land Beyond! Where and Oh where can Gandalf and the dwarfs have got to? I only hope to goodness they are not still back there in the power of the goblins!"

He still wandered on, out of the little high valley, over its edge, and down the slopes beyond; but all the while a very uncomfortable thought was growing inside him. He wondered whether he ought not, now he had the magic ring, to go back into the horrible, horrible tunnels and look for his friends. He had just made up his mind that it was his duty, that he must turn back – and very miserable he felt about it – when he heard voices.

He stopped and listened. It did not sound like goblins; so he crept forward carefully. He was on a stony path winding downwards with a rocky wall on the left hand; on the other side the ground sloped away and there were dells below the level of the path overhung with bushes and low trees. In one of these dells under the bushes people were talking.

He crept still nearer, and suddenly he saw peering between two big boulders a head with a red hood on: it was Balin doing look-out. He could have clapped and shouted for joy, but he did not. He had still got the ring on, for fear of meeting something unexpected and unpleasant, and he saw that Balin was looking straight at him without noticing him.

"I will give them all a surprise," he thought, as he crawled into the bushes at the edge of the dell.

from 'The Hobbit' by J.R.R. Tolkien

Understanding

A Answer these questions about the first three paragraphs. Explain how the passage helped you to choose each answer.

1 Where had Bilbo been and what had happened to him?
2 How did he find out where he was?
3 Who were his friends and where did he think they were?
4 Why did the goblins worry him so much?
5 What did he decide to do?

B Now use the rest of the passage to answer these questions.

1 What made Bilbo stop?
2 Who do you think Balin was?
3 What do you now know was the power of the magic ring?
4 Why didn't Bilbo call out?
5 How do the last two paragraphs show Bilbo's change of mood?

My own work

A Make up a story about Bilbo's adventures just before the passage begins. Include in your story the goblins, Bilbo's friends, the magic ring and the horrible tunnels.

B Everyone would like a magic ring that would make you invisible when you wore it. Imagine you had a magic ring for a day and wore it at home and in school. Write an account of what happened.

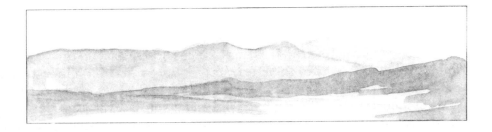

Not all rings are like Bilbo's magic ring. Those in the picture contain different jewels to make them attractive. Below are ten minerals and gems that are used in rings. Find information in the library about where each of them is found, their colour, size and value. Use the information to make a booklet that a jeweller might use to help his customers choose their rings.

gold	silver	diamond	ruby	sapphire
emerald	opal	pearl	amethyst	garnet

Words

A   When the prefix <u>un</u> is added to an adjective, it makes a word opposite in meaning. An example from the passage is <u>uncomfortable</u>. Write down the two other examples in the passage and three more words with the same prefix.

B   <u>Dis</u>, <u>mis</u>, <u>in</u> and <u>non</u> are prefixes that have the same effect as <u>un</u>. They make words that are opposite in meaning to the original word. So does the suffix <u>less</u>. Write down two more words to add to each of the examples below.

dis . . .	dislike
mis . . .	misprint
in . . .	inaccurate
non . . .	nonsense
. . . less	tasteless

Language

The main **parts of speech** are nouns, verbs, adjectives, adverbs, conjunctions, pronouns and prepositions. Find each of the following in the passage.

1 the six **nouns** that name the things Bilbo had lost
2 one **proper noun** that names a person and two proper nouns that name a place
3 the **adjective** used twice to describe the tunnels
4 one other **adjective** and the **noun** (or **pronoun**) it describes
5 the last **verb**
6 the three **prepositions** that introduce phrases **after** the last verb
7 the three **pronouns** in the last paragraph (one of them used twice)
8 the **conjunction** in the last paragraph
9 two **adverbs**, near the beginning of the fourth paragraph, that give more information on **how** and **where** Bilbo crept
10 one other **adverb**

Bats

A bat is born
Naked and blind and pale.
His mother makes a pocket of her tail
And catches him. He clings to her long fur
By his thumbs and toes and teeth.
And then the mother dances through the night
Doubling and looping, soaring, somersaulting –
Her baby hangs on underneath.
All night, in happiness, she hunts and flies.
Her high sharp cries
Like shining needlepoints of sound
Go out into the night and, echoing back,
Tell her what they have touched.
She hears how far it is, how big it is,
Which way it's going:
She lives by hearing.
The mother eats the moths and gnats she catches
In full flight; in full flight
The mother drinks the water of the pond
She skims across. Her baby hangs on tight.
Her baby drinks the milk she makes him
In moonlight or starlight, in mid-air.
Their single shadow, printed on the moon
Or fluttering across the stars,
Whirls on all night; at daybreak
The tired mother flaps home to her rafter.
The others all are there.
They hang themselves up by their toes;
They wrap themselves in their brown wings.
Bunched upside-down, they sleep in air.
Their sharp ears, their sharp teeth, their quick sharp faces
Are dull and slow and mild.
All the bright day, as the mother sleeps,
She folds her wings about her sleeping child.

Randall Jarrel

Understanding

A   Make a list of all the features of a bat's life and behaviour described in the poem. Include such things as the way it flies and what it eats as well as how it looks after its young.

B   Now use your list for a piece of writing with the title 'A baby bat's night'. Do not look at the poem again until you have finished writing and then compare what you have written with the poem.

My own work

A   Choose any other wild animal or pet you know. Describe a day or a night in the life of this creature.

B   Now use your description to write a piece of poetry, about ten lines long, about the animal you have chosen.

Different species of bats are found all over the world. Below is a list of five species, each of which may be found in the continent named in brackets. Ask your teacher for an outline map of the world or trace one yourself from an atlas. Mark the name of each of the species of bat in the correct region on your map.

pipistrelle (Europe)   horseshoe bat (Africa)
fish-eating bat (Asia)   vampire bat (South America)
flying fox (Australia)

Words

A **participle** ends in <u>ing</u> or <u>ed</u> and is formed from a verb. Look at the seventh line of the poem in which the poet chose four participles to describe the flight of the bat.

Choose two good participles to describe each of the following.

1 the wind on a breezy day
2 a diamond
3 leaves in autumn
4 a crowd at a football match
5 a gymnast doing floor exercises
6 storm clouds
7 a baby in a pram
8 waves on a rocky coast
9 freshly fallen snow
10 an athlete at the end of a race

Language

A   The poem might have been written out as **prose** and not in lines of **poetry**, but the **rhythm** and occasional **rhymes** help to make it **verse**.

Choose each of the following from the poem and write them out.

1 two consecutive lines that rhyme with each other
2 two lines that rhyme with each other but are separated by other lines
3 three lines that have a pleasant or regular rhythm
4 two effective short lines
5 two lines that run together to form a complete sentence

B   As well as the rhythm, the rhyme and the different line lengths, the poem is made successful by the images or pictures it creates in your mind. Choose three lines that you think are successful in this way.

The ruined village

By nightfall, foot-sore and hungry, the boys halted on the moorland path which they had followed for most of the day, to see a red glow flickering in the sky. The sullen orange-red hues were reflected from the underside of dark clouds which seemed to stretch over that part of the countryside, making the early evening ominous, almost frightening. Gwydion said grimly, "We do not need to ask the direction of Mai Dun now. That is the last of the fortress, and of the village at its foot."

Gaius said, "Have my people, the Romans, done this, do you think?"

Gwydion shook his head. "It might just as easily have been the Belgae. They would not leave a fortress whole if they left it; which means that either way, we have been defeated."

Gaius put his hand on his friend's arm as though to show that among friends there is no such thing as nationality or race. Gwydion smiled back at him, though a little sadly, and thought that if all Celts and Romans were like this, war would be impossible between them.

Then stumbling now, from fatigue and the roughness of the road, they began their melancholy journey towards the burning stronghold, wondering what they might find when at last they reached the place of battle.

The moon was high, when they reached the ruined earthworks, and shone down eerily upon tumbled men and horses who lay here and there upon the ground, throwing a gentle silver light upon this sad carnage, picking out here a raised hand, there a broken helmet; throwing a malicious illumination over things which seemed to cry out for secrecy and peace. High on the summit of the hill, the ruined fortress occasion-ally threw up a transient glow of light, as some last beam or stretch of thatch caught fire, and burned itself to an ember. The battle was over, and now across the broad and undulating field, men and even women were moving slowly, some of them carrying torches, seeking their dead, or tearing off the finery of those who were helpless to resist them.

Of the Romans or the Belgae, there were no signs now. It seemed that the tide of battle had swept on and that the field of Mai Dun was already forgotten history.

from 'Legions of the Eagle' by Henry Treece

Understanding

1 Although Gaius and Gwydion were friends, their peoples were enemies. To which race did each belong?
2 How do you know the boys had been on a long journey?
3 What caused the red glow in the sky?
4 What was Mai Dun and what do you think was Gwydion's connection with it?
5 Why did Gwydion think it would not matter whether it was the Romans or the Belgae who had defeated his people?
6 What made the battlefield easy to see when they reached it?
7 Why couldn't the boys tell who had won the battle?
8 In what condition was the fortress at the top of the hill?
9 What were the other people doing on the battlefield?
10 Why is the last sentence a sad one?

My own work

A   Imagine you had been **either** a soldier in the battle of Mai Dun **or** a spectator watching from the hills around. Write an account of what happened to you or what you saw.

B   The next to last paragraph of the passage describes the scene after the battle. Newspaper reports often describe the scene after a disaster such as a flood or earthquake. Imagine you are a reporter who arrives at the scene of one of these disasters some time after it has happened. Write your newspaper report, giving it a suitable headline.

The passage describes the time of the Roman occupation of Britain,
and the picture shows what Hadrian's Wall was like at that time. Here
are three topics on which to find information and write some notes.

1 the Roman invasion of Britain
2 the life of a Roman soldier
3 Hadrian's Wall

Make each of the topics into a chapter of a book on the Roman
occupation of Britain. Include diagrams and drawings where suitable
and make an attractive cover for your book. Write an introduction and
include a contents page and index.

Words

The passage contains a number of difficult words. You probably guessed the meaning of these words from the **context** (the words around that help you to understand the general sense).

Here are ten words from the passage. Find them and write down what you think they mean. Then check your answers in a dictionary.

sullen	ominous	fatigue	melancholy	eerily
carnage	malicious	transient	ember	undulating

Language revision

1 Look at the first sentence of the passage. In what ways is it a good opening sentence for the first paragraph?
2 Write down three **compound nouns** from the first paragraph.
3 Write down the plurals of <u>fortress</u> (third paragraph), <u>nationality</u> (fourth paragraph) and <u>journey</u> (fifth paragraph).
4 Look at the two words <u>friend's</u> and <u>friends</u> in the fourth paragraph. Why is there an **apostrophe** in the first but not the second word?
5 In the last sentence of the fourth paragraph Gwydion thought about the Celts and the Romans. How would the author have written out his thought if he had said it aloud to Gaius?
6 From **each** of the last five paragraphs write down one word with a letter, or letters, unsounded.
7 Explain the spelling rule obeyed by the ending of the word <u>occasionally</u> in the next to the last paragraph.
8 Write down a suitable title for the topic of the last paragraph.
9 Why does the author use the word <u>tide</u> in the last paragraph, to describe the battle?
10 Write a sentence of your own about the friendship of Gwydion and Gaius.

Thinking about a ghost

James decided to wait until the evening. If you have something important to say there is no point, he'd learned from experience, in saying it during the most active part of the day when people are coming home and getting meals and eating them and whatever you are trying to say gets lost in a commotion of doors opening and shutting and crockery banging and people asking where the newspaper is. He'd tested that out before now: he'd stood in the middle of the kitchen and said, "I broke my leg at school today," and his mother had turned the hot tap on and put another pile of plates in the sink and said, "Yes, dear. I'll see about it tomorrow, dear." No, it would be better to wait till later, when the household had subsided a little, come off the boil, so to speak, when his parents would be relaxed and more receptive.

Having spent an hour or so being helpful and unobtrusive, and especially friendly towards Helen, making tender enquiries about what sort of day she'd had and so forth, so that she wouldn't be in a spiky interrupting mood, he retreated to the apple tree, for a spell of rest and contemplation. He took the Personal Notebook with him, and began to fill it in; life must go on, no matter how large your problems may be. 'Pocket money,' he wrote. 'Situation as before. Emergency reserve now down to two lollies and one gob-stopper. Weather: Windy inside and out. Black beetles come out earlier now – is it because it gets dark earlier? Note: do scientific research on this. Could I put numbers on beetles with white paint? – no, cruel, I think. Will just have to watch carefully. Future plans: Find out more about poltergeists, if poss.' Here it occurred to him that such openness might be unwise. If Thomas Kempe could write presumably he could read; James crossed out 'poltergeists' and wrote 'you-know-what'. 'Do other people have them and if so how do they get rid of them?' He changed his mind, crossed out 'get rid of them', and substituted 'get them altered'. This might be excessively cautious, but you didn't want him getting suspicious. He turned over the page and continued, 'Excavate rubbish workmen threw out: let Simon join in maybe. Store apples somewhere in case I starve in the winter. Borrow biscuit from larder later and see if mice can be tamed. If so, train mice to carry messages. Find out if big chestnut tree in churchyard is climbable and if so climb it.'

from 'The Ghost of Thomas Kempe' by Penelope Lively

Understanding

A 1 James had something important to say to his parents. Why did he decide to wait until evening?
   2 Who do you think Helen was and why was James so pleasant to her?
   3 Why did James go into the garden?
   4 Who or what do you think Thomas Kempe was?
   5 Why was James very careful what he wrote in the notebook about poltergeists?

B What have you learned from the passage about James's hobbies and interests?

My own work

A James kept a Personal Notebook in which he wrote down his thoughts on all sorts of things and his plans for the future. Write out a page of **your** Personal Notebook, using the same type of method that James used.

B The passage makes it clear that later in the evening James hoped to tell his parents about his problem, probably something to do with the poltergeist, Thomas Kempe. Write out the conversation they had, in the form of a **play**. Remember that Helen would also be present.

James kept a Personal Notebook and the picture shows the pages of a diary, another type of book for recording events and appointments. Diaries also contain a page of personal information about the owner and details of such things as addresses, public holidays, times of sunset, etc.

Make yourself a diary to begin on the first day of next month and fill in any important dates you need to remember. Include some pages of information of the type mentioned above. During the month use your diary to note down important events that have happened.

Sentences

Look at the way James wrote in his Personal Notebook. He often wrote his ideas in **note form**, with only the most important words of a sentence included. For example, when he wrote about his pocket money he put, 'Pocket money. Situation as before.'

Write a few words in note form about each of the following.

1   the weather today
2   breakfast this morning
3   your journey to school today
4   your mood at the moment
5   what you have been doing during the last hour
6   something you are planning to do later
7   a problem you have to overcome
8   your best friend
9   a record you particularly like
10 some news you have heard recently

Language revision

1   Look at the first sentence of the passage. Why is it a good opening sentence for the first paragraph?
2   Write down five **participles** used in the second sentence of the passage.
3   Write down three words from the passage in which an **apostrophe** is used to show a letter has been omitted. How would each word have been written without an apostrophe and in full?
4   Explain what the author meant when she used the expression come off the boil in the last sentence of the first paragraph.
5   Write down a word in the second paragraph that uses the **prefix** un to form an **antonym** of the original word.
6   Explain the spelling rules obeyed by the words helpful and friendly in the first sentence of the second paragraph.
7   Look at the sentence in the second paragraph beginning, 'He changed his mind ....' Write down two **synonyms** of changed from the same paragraph.
8   Look at the sentence in the second paragraph beginning, 'Store apples . . .' Which word in this sentence would be wrongly spelt as two words? Which two words would be wrongly spelt as one word?
9   Write a sentence to explain what a poltergeist is.
10 Choose one of the statements James wrote in note form and rewrite it as a complete sentence.

Book list

Richard Adams	Watership Down (Rex Collings)
Gillian Avery	Ellen and the Queen (Hamish Hamilton)
Nina Bawden	Squib (Gollancz)
Elisabeth Beresford	The Wombles at Work (Ernest Benn)
Paul Biegel	The Little Captain (Dent)
Lucy M. Boston	The Chimneys of Green Knowe (Faber & Faber)
Helen Cresswell	The Night Watchmen (Faber & Faber)
Alan Garner	The Weirdstone of Brisingamen (Collins)
Eve Garnett	Holiday at the Dew Drop Inn (Heinemann)
Jean Craighead George ..	Julie of the Wolves (Hamish Hamilton)
Susan Hale	Painter's Mate (Methuen)
Geraldine Kaye	Nowhere to Stop (Hodder & Stoughton)
Carol Kendall	The Minnipins (Dent)
Penelope Lively	The Ghost of Thomas Kempe (Heinemann)
A. Rutgers van der Loeff ..	Children on the Oregon Trail (Hodder & Stoughton)
Richard Parker	Paul and Etta (Hodder & Stoughton)
Philippa Pearce	Tom's Midnight Garden (Oxford University Press)
Dodie Smith	The Hundred and One Dalmatians (Heinemann)
Noel Streatfeild	The Growing Summer (Collins)
Elizabeth Stucley	Magnolia Buildings (Bodley Head)
Robert Tibber	Aristide (Hutchinson)
J.R.R. Tolkien	The Hobbit (Allen & Unwin)
Henry Treece	Legions of the Eagle (Bodley Head)
Jay Williams, Ray Abrashkin..	Danny Dunn – Time Traveller (Macdonald & Jane's)

Acknowledgements

Thanks are due to the following publishers, agents and authors for permission to reprint the copyright material indicated. Every effort has been made to trace the ownership of all copyright material. Should any question arise as to the use of any extract, or any error, it is hoped that the publishers will be informed.

Hamish Hamilton Ltd. for extracts from *Ellen and the Queen* by Gillian Avery and *Julie of the Wolves* by Jean Craighead George; Hutchinson Publishing Group Ltd. for an extract from *Aristide* by Robert Tibber; Methuen Children's Books Ltd. for an extract from *Painter's Mate* by Susan Hale; Hodder & Stoughton Children's Books Ltd. for extracts from *Paul and Etta* by Richard Parker, *Children on the Oregon Trail* by A. Rutgers van der Loeff, and *Nowhere to Stop* by Geraldine Kaye; J.M. Dent & Sons Ltd. for extracts from *The Little Captain* by Paul Biegel, and *The Minnipins* by Carol Kendall; the Estate of the late Richard Church for the poem *The Woodpecker* by Richard Church, from *The Inheritors*, published by Heinemann; Ernest Benn Ltd. for an extract from *The Wombles at Work* by Elisabeth Beresford; Oxford University Press for an extract from *Tom's Midnight Garden* by A. Philippa Pearce (1958); William Heinemann Ltd. for extracts from *The Hundred and One Dalmatians* by Dodie Smith, *Holiday at the Dew Drop Inn* by Eve Garnett, and *The Ghost of Thomas Kempe* by Penelope Lively; Vernon Scannell for the poem *Hide and Seek*, published in the BBC pamphlet *Listening and Writing* (1973); Victor Gollancz Ltd. for an extract from *Squib* by Nina Bawden; William Collins Sons & Co Ltd. for *The Weirdstone of Brisingamen* by Alan Garner, and *The Growing Summer* by Noel Streatfeild; Rex Collings Ltd., London, for an extract from *Watership Down* by Richard Adams; Blackie & Son Ltd. for the poem *All Along the Street* by F.J. Teskey; Macdonald & Jane's Publishers Ltd. for an extract from *Danny Dunn – Time Traveller* by Jay Williams and Ray Abrashkin, Faber and Faber Ltd. for extracts from *The Night Watchmen* by Helen Cresswell, *The Chimneys of Green Knowe* by Lucy M. Boston, and the poem *My Father* from *Meet My Folks* by Ted Hughes; The Bodley Head Ltd. for extracts from *Magnolia Buildings* by Elizabeth Stucley, and *Legions of the Eagle* by Henry Treece; George Allen & Unwin (Publishers) Ltd. for an extract from *The Hobbit* by J.R.R. Tolkien; Penguin Books Ltd. for the poem *A Bat is Born* from *Randall Jarrell: the Bat-Poet* (Kestrel Books, 1977) pp. 36–7 © 1963, 1964 by the Macmillan Publishing Co. Inc.